Performance Appraisals in Business and Industry

Key to Effective Supervision

George L. Morrisey

President, MOR Associates
Buena Park, California

ADDISON-WESLEY PUBLISHING COMPANY

Reading, Massachusetts • Menlo Park, California

London • Amsterdam • Don Mills, Ontario • Sydney

Library of Congress Cataloging in Publication Data

Morrisey, George L.
  Performance appraisals in business and industry.

  Bibliography: p. 143
  1. Employees, Rating of—United States. I. Title.
HF5549.5.R3M67   1983   658.3′125   83–6035
ISBN 0-201-04831-0

ISBN 0-201-04831-0
ABCDEFGHIJ-AL-89876543

Preface

WHY WAS THIS BOOK WRITTEN?

The original version of this book, *Appraisal and Development through Objectives and Results* (Addison-Wesley, 1972), was written largely out of my experience as a trainer and a manager in two aerospace companies (Rockwell and Douglas) and one federal government organization (U.S. Postal Service). Many of the concepts and techniques discussed in that book are equally valid today and have been included in this edition as well, with only slight modifications.

However, there have been some significant changes that have taken place in the period since that book was published, both in the legal ramifications of the performance appraisal process and in my own perceptions as a consultant working with thousands of managers in hundreds of organizations in both the public and private sectors. As a result, this book is being published simultaneously in two editions—this one directed to managers in business and industry and another one to managers in governmental organizations.

There has been a substantial amount of legislation in the past decade that has had a profound effect on performance appraisals. The single most significant one was the Civil Service Reform Act of 1978 which radically changed the requirements for performance appraisals in most federal agencies and which has had considerable "ripple" effect on state and local governments and in the private sector as well. In addition, legislation and court decisions related to equal opportunity, discrimination, flexible age retirement, disclosure of information, etc., have placed organizations and individual supervisors on notice that performance appraisals can no longer be treated as the "annual Personnel paperwork exercise" as perceived by many, if not most, members of management.

This book addresses these issues head on and provides some solid "how to" approaches to meeting the new requirements while still retaining the heavy emphasis on performance appraisal as a developmental more than a "score-keeping" tool. It expands on the appraisal models developed in the original text and provides several additional alternatives that can be adapted to fit virtually any organizational requirement for performance appraisal. More than that, it provides practical guidance on how to make this tool the "key to effective supervision."

FOR WHOM IS THIS BOOK WRITTEN?

This book is designed as a guide for individual members of management at all levels, from the top on down. The generic term *supervisor* is used throughout to describe anyone who supervises the performance of others and has the responsibility for reviewing their performance. We have separate chapters devoted to appraising managers and individual employees, acknowledging both the similarities and the differences in applying the process to each. We have deliberately avoided recommending specific appraisal forms and organizational policies on the assumption that the vast majority of readers must respond to whatever forms and policies are established. Although based on the principles of Management by Objectives and Results, a manager need not be formally involved in MOR (MBO) to make this approach to performance appraisal work. Naturally, our bias suggests that the performance appraisal process is likely to be more effective in those organizations practicing MOR as a way to manage.

A WORD ABOUT SEXISM

I was convinced several years ago by some of my feminist colleagues to adopt a writing and speaking style that eliminates male-dominant language. (This is a departure from the original version of this book which is replete with male pronouns.) Once I conditioned myself to thinking in this vein, it was easier to change my writing style than I had anticipated. You should be able to read this book without having to translate between genders.

HOW CAN THIS BOOK BE USED?

This book is designed primarily as a *text for an organizational training program* on performance appraisals. Several effective approaches to conducting such training are described in the *Instructor's Guide*, which is available separately from the publisher.

For use as an *individual study guide* for the working manager or student of management, we make these recommendations:

1. Read the Preface, Chapters 1 and 2, plus Chapter 11 for an overview of the philosophy and process. If you are not already familiar with the concepts related to Management by Objectives and Results, then you may wish to read Chapter 3, "MOR Revisited."

2. Determine which of the following alternatives best serves your individual needs:
   a) Selective learning of specific concepts and techniques to supplement your existing knowledge
   b) Concentrating on the use of the various appraisal models, including the use of performance standards, as applied to individual employees and/or managers
   c) Concentrating on the communication skills needed for using performance appraisal as a developmental tool
   d) Learning, adapting, and applying the entire process to your areas of responsibility

3. If you have selected 2(a) as most appropriate for you, the recommendation is easy. Study and, where appropriate, practice those concepts and techniques that will satisfy this need. A word of caution, however: you should be aware that some of the concepts and techniques may not work as effectively outside the total context that is being recommended here.

4. If 2(b) seems best for you at the moment, Chapters 4, 5, and 6 will be of most value to you. We recommend that you start with your own job, applying whichever approach appears most useful, before applying it to any of the people or positions reporting to you. Then we suggest that you discuss the various alternatives with at least some, if not all, of your direct reports to get their cooperation and to reach agreement on the most effective approach.

5. If 2(c) is the area that has the most appeal for you now, Chapters 7, 8, and 9 should be the section on which you concentrate. Remember, of course, that reading about these concepts and techniques and applying them are quite different. Practice in a low-risk situation is essential to effective learning here. This is why we recommend role playing or some other form of applied practice in any kind of formal training effort.

6. If you are ready to commit yourself to 2(d), then we recommend working through the book a chapter at a time, discussing it with your supervisor, your direct reports, and your peer managers, as appropriate. When you reach Chapter 4, you should begin to apply the models to your own job, possibly at the same time others are applying it to theirs. Practice each of the concepts and techniques at every opportunity. The only way to develop these skills is to use them.

7. Use the book as a continual reference to reinforce your learning and to test the validity of whatever approach you are using.

8. Don't get discouraged when you hit the inevitable periods of setback and frustration in applying the concepts and techniques discussed in this book. Stay with it, and both your satisfaction and your effectiveness as a supervisor will increase as you continue to develop your skills.

Acknowledgments

Thanks go to the many managers, in both the public and private sectors, who have participated in my seminars and to those managers and trainers who have given me direct feedback on my writings, for forcing me to refine this approach to performance appraisal to the point where it now can be truly a "key to effective supervision." I am particularly grateful to the following professionals for their continued inspiration and assistance:

Peter Drucker and *George Odiorne*, two "giants" who have influenced me in so many ways and who continue to come up with some of the most creative and practical ideas for making the art of management truly effective;

My partner, *Fred Clark*, for his creative ideas and practical feedback and, even more importantly, for his marvelous ability to force me to practice what I preach;

The following colleagues at North American Aviation (now Rockwell International) and Douglas Aircraft Company who helped in the development of some of the concepts covered in the original version of this book: *Wally Gass, George Hedden, Bob Himes, Dave Lewis, Dick Rinella, Jack Rush, Tom Scobel, Bill Weingartner,* and *Bill Wellstead;*

Bill Guthrie, of Guthrie Associates, who helped polish some of the earlier material and who published an earlier version of portions of that book for use in some programs we did together;

Mory Bryson, of Bryson Associates, for his ideas and information related to documentation and for his appendix article on that subject.

Buena Park, California   G.L.M.
January 1983

Contents

1

Introduction

The need for a truly effective and meaningful performance appraisal process in virtually every employing organization has never been greater than it is today. The increasing legal and human implications of such a process are becoming more evident as challenges to personnel actions are approaching near-epidemic stages. The impact of various types of legislation related to equal employment opportunity, affirmative action, flexible age retirement, disclosure laws, etc., on all types of employing organizations can be enormous.

While upper management in most organizations readily acknowledges the need for increased attention in this important area, relatively few have addressed it as an integral part of the total management process. The result frequently is a new policy and procedure document (prepared by staff people with little input from line organizations) containing lofty philosophical statements and a series of "thou shalts" and "thou shalt nots," accompanied by a new set of forms. The poor supervisor, the individual required to make the process work, sees it primarily as one more administrative burden which carries little or no personal benefit and for which he or she is ill-prepared.

The irony of recent developments, of course, is that so much emphasis has been placed on the *negative* impact of *not doing* an effective job of performance appraisal that we tend to lose sight of the much greater *positive* impact of *doing* an effective job in this critical area of supervision. Furthermore, it is a process that can and, in fact, must be beneficial to the individual supervisor. And it can be accomplished through the use of discrete skills that *can be learned* by most people with supervisory responsibility. These skills are concentrated in three primary areas: performance measurement criteria, interpersonal communications (before, during, and after the performance measurement period), and documentation. This book will address what both the organization and the individual supervisor must do in order for an effective performance appraisal process to succeed. (The term *supervisor* with a small *s*

1

will be used throughout to describe any individual, regardless of his or her position in the organizational hierarchy, who has responsibility for the performance of others.)

BENEFITS OF AN EFFECTIVE PERFORMANCE APPRAISAL PROCESS

As any experienced sales person will recognize, benefits fall under two general categories: value added and loss avoided. Since "loss avoided" generally has more direct emotional appeal than "value added," we will address that category first, followed by "value added," initially for the organization and then for the individual supervisor and, finally, for the individual employee or supervisee.

For the Organization

Loss avoided

Reduced liability for potential legal action related to noncompliance, discrimination, or "reverse" discrimination in personnel actions

Reduced cost of litigation

Reduced loss of organizational image through "bad press"

Reduced employee turnover

Reduced losses resulting from ineffective performance, gross negligence, or willful misconduct

Value added

Improved over-all productivity

More effective and efficient use of personnel

Improved organizational results

Improved internal communications

Greater attraction to potential new employees

More motivated employees

Improved potential for the future

Recognized compliance with the various related federal, state, and local laws

For the Individual Supervisor

Loss avoided

Avoidance of possible personal legal and financial liability as a result of improper personnel actions

Reduction or elimination of adverse personnel actions due to poor communications

Reduction of criticism from higher level management for what may be perceived as poor supervision

Reduction of nonproductive or counterproductive conflict with and among employees being supervised

Reduction of stress over conflicts related to employee improvement through use of regular progress reviews

Value added

Improved performance by those being supervised

Better personal performance rating because of improved performance of those being supervised (presumably resulting in greater personal reward and recognition)

More stable work group

Increased group morale and productivity

Better understanding and agreement related to group and individual expectations

Positive method for coping with marginal performance

A feeling of being "in control"

Better qualified replacements for key positions (including that of the supervisor when a promotional opportunity comes along)

For the Individual Employee (Supervisee)

Loss avoided

Avoidance of possible loss of advancement, increased compensation, or employment because of a lack of understanding of job expectations or of current performance compared to those expectations

Decreased likelihood of being given undesirable assignments

Reduction of conflict with supervisor and co-workers

Reduction or elimination of the frustration from not knowing "where I stand"

Value added

Better picture of where he or she is going, career-wise

Clear understanding of supervisor's expectations

Continuous update of performance against those expectations

Greater personal reward and recognition for meeting those expectations

Greater personal satisfaction

Opportunity to increase capability and value through agreed-upon development plan

Opportunity to contribute more directly to organizational as well as personal improvement

DEPARTURES FROM TRADITION

There have been some distinct shifts in management philosophy related to performance appraisal by some organizations in recent years, as reflected in The Conference Board's 1977 Research Report.[1] The research was conducted among 293 corporations representing a broad spectrum of industries, including large companies as well as some with under 1,000 employees. We will reference some of these findings in our comments. However, many performance appraisal efforts still remain relatively ineffective because of an easy-way-out continuation of certain traditional practices. Let's examine a few of the departures from traditional practices that need to be instituted if this approach to performance appraisal is to be truly effective.

Relationship of Objective to Subjective Measures.   The graduated checklists, wherein a supervisor is asked to rate an employee on a scale of 1 to 5 (or some other numerical range) on obviously important characteristics such as initiative, loyalty, dependability, leadership, etc., are as familiar as an old shoe to most supervisors who have been functioning in that role for any significant length of time. The only problem with these checklists is that, to our knowledge, no one has yet come up with a method for (1) defining these characteristics in terms that will have a common and consistent meaning for all who must relate to them; (2) assessing the relative importance, if any, of these characteristics to on-the-job performance; (3) assuring consistency of rating among supervisors (or even of the same supervisor at different times); or (4) determining whether or not these factors actually correlate with "good management." The upshot is that even the most conscientious supervisor must rely almost entirely on a "gut feel" approach to evaluation. In effect, we end up playing God with an employee's career on the basis of little more than a personal opinion.

The real problem with subjective forms of measurement is that they tend to evaluate what an individual *is* and *knows* more than what he or she *does*. Objective measures, on the other hand, concern themselves primarily with *performance,* which is really what the appraisal process is all about. To be sure, objective measures are much more difficult to establish than subjective ones, but, once done, they can provide a valid and reliable yardstick for evaluation and development purposes. Furthermore, there is still ample room for making value judgments (which are subjective) in selecting what should be measured and in determining what external factors might influence the results. The establishment of key results areas, objectives, and standards as recommended in this book and many contemporary personnel policies does not remove the judgment factor from the process. Rather, it enhances it.

The Conference Board Report indicates that more and more organizations are recognizing the importance of a more objective approach and, in fact, profess to be following one, as reflected in Table 1.1.

In spite of the fact that a large number of companies *report* that they follow an *"objective setting or MBO"* approach, there is an apparent inconsistency with actual practice. "One hundred and twenty-five company appraisal forms were received; fully a third do not seem to correspond in approach to the approach reported on the accompanying questionnaire. . . . Thus, in spite

Table 1.1 Company approaches to performance appraisal

	Lower management (217 companies)		Middle management (208 companies)		Top management (160 companies)	
	Number of companies	Percent of companies	Number of companies	Percent of companies	Number of companies	Percent of companies
Objective Setting or MBO	87	40%	110	53%	100	63%
Essay	81	37	76	37	58	36
Ratings Conventional or graphic	37	17	33	16	16	10
Behaviorally anchored	20	9	17	8	14	9
Critical Incident	33	15	30	14	17	11
Checklists Behavioral	28	13	23	11	13	8
Trait	29	13	23	11	14	9
Forced choice	11	5	9	4	4	2
Rankings or Comparisons Straight ranking	14	6	16	8	8	5
Alternation ranking	4	2	4	2	1	0.6
Forced distribution	32	15	28	13	16	10
Paired comparison	2	1	4	2	1	0.6

Robert I. Lazer and Walter S. Wikstrom, *Appraising Managerial Performance: Current Practices and Future Directions.* Conference Board Report No. 723, copyright 1977.

of what Table [1.1] shows, it is possible that the conventional rating scale is the most commonly used approach to managerial performance appraisal.''[2] It appears that many of the problems most organizations are having in implementing performance appraisal systems are similar to those experienced in many of the companies surveyed. While we feel it is still absolutely essential to come up with measurable performance factors to make the appraisal process work in any type of organization, perhaps there is some consolation in knowing that it has not been easy to develop these in those companies covered in the survey either.

Having made our plea for objectivity, let's back off for a moment and establish a case for some subjective analysis as well. In an article in the *Harvard Business Review,* Harry Levinson pointed out some of the potential weaknesses in the management-by-objectives process as it relates to performance appraisal. In analyzing the emphasis on objectivity, he states:

> Every organization is a social system, a network of interpersonal relationships. [An individual] may do an excellent job by objective standards of measurement, but may fail miserably as a partner, subordinate, superior or colleague. It is a commonplace that more people fail to be promoted for personal reasons than for technical inadequacy. . . . The plea for objectivity is vain for another reason. The greater the emphasis on measurement and quantification, the more likely the subtle nonmeasurable elements of the task will be sacrificed. Quality of performance frequently, therefore, loses out to quantification.[3]

Levinson makes a valid point in this regard. A too strict by-the-book approach to quantifiable objectives as the *only* method of measurement may prove to have very little more value than the old personality checklists. In spite of the convenience of having a purely quantifiable scale from which an arithmetic ''score'' can be computed, we must consider the human element, which is not always measurable in an objective sense.

Every performance appraisal (particularly at higher levels of management) needs to have some subjective analysis of those performance factors that do not readily lend themselves to objective measurement. However, this subjective analysis must be directed toward what the employee *does* rather than what the employee *is.* Rather than having ''an irritating personality,'' an employee's ''behavior causes others to avoid direct contact.'' Furthermore, the judgments arrived at in this manner can, and in fact must, be supported by objective data. The behavior being described must clearly be a major factor related to the achievement or nonachievement of objectives. (The fact that other people may ''avoid direct contact'' is of little importance unless those ''other people'' *must* interface with the individual being appraised in order to satisfactorily complete their jobs.)

Therefore, in discussing the relationship between objective and subjective measures, we are not talking about an ''either/or'' situation. What we are saying is that, to have any value for either evaluation or development purposes, attention must be directed to performance rather than personality, and the basis for evaluation must be made as objective as possible with any subjective judgments based on objective observations.

Tailored Rather than Standard Approach. One of the "ideals" that many organizations have been looking for is a universal or standard approach to performance appraisal with a common appraisal form that is equally applicable throughout the organization. I took a position in the initial version of this book that "we have yet to see, nor can we envisage, either an approach or a form that would be equally meaningful to managers in, say, production, engineering, sales and accounting." I am now prepared to modify that position based on some of the organizational approaches I have seen, recognizing that "equally meaningful" may not be attainable in a literal sense.

The key to the modification in my position here is the realization that *universal* and *tailored* are not necessarily incompatible terms. Several organizations (including some illustrated in the earlier-referenced Conference Board Report) have taken a management-by-objectives-related approach, together with an accompanying form, that allows for specific tailoring to both the position and the incumbent. We will demonstrate in Chapter 4 how to develop a performance appraisal model that is specifically tailored to individual job requirements while still functioning within a universal approach.

Performance Appraisal Rather than the Multipurpose Evaluation. Most supervisors are periodically required to evaluate the employees reporting to them for such things as salary determination, promotions, layoffs, reassignments, and disciplinary action, as well as for development purposes. How convenient it is if we can cover all these bases with a single formal appraisal! How naive we are if we honestly believe that we can effectively accomplish them all with one effort. The purposes of each, and the accompanying roles of the supervisor are quite different. The Conference Board Report further bears this out: "When, as a part of this survey, a panel of 25 managers for various human resource activities was asked to generate a list of problems encountered with performance appraisal systems, the first item mentioned was 'conflicting multiple uses.' " The results of their research show "that more than three-quarters of the companies responding to this question use their performance appraisals for three or more purposes. Further, more than 30 percent of the companies report that they try to accommodate five or more uses with their appraisals."[4] This, of course, is one of the major stumbling blocks to the effective implementation of performance appraisal systems.

Salary review, for example, serves two primary purposes—to provide tangible recognition for past performance, and to determine a fair rate of pay for services rendered. But, it is related almost entirely to the past with its future implications tied only to the rather nebulous motivational impact of the decisions reached. "After all," the employee rationalizes after having been given a salary increase, "it's what is due me for the work I have done." If no increase is given or if it is less than the employee anticipated, the employee's reaction is likely to be quite negative. Consequently, in neither situation is salary review an appropriate time to realistically examine development needs. By all means, the use of objectives and results for salary review purposes is both valid and highly desirable. (We'll have more to say about this in Chapter 10.) The approach, however, is quite different from that used in some of the other applications of the performance appraisal process.

Promotion, on the other hand, while looking at past performance, examines it in light of the requirements in a new position. Thus, as any effective supervisor knows, the top performer in a particular job is not necessarily the best candidate for the next higher position. The use of objectives and results, once again, is extremely helpful when applied selectively to those areas of past performance that are indicators of potential performance in the new job.

When looking at possible requirements for *layoff* (this is becoming more of a reality in governmental organizations) or *reassignment,* assuming that seniority is not the primary consideration, we examine the individual's past performance in terms of future skill needs. Tangible measurement of performance, as is possible by use of objectives and results, can substantially reduce the possibility of emotional decisions at such times.

Performance appraisal, when used as a basis for *disciplinary action,* requires careful documentation of specific courses of action mutually agreed to or, perhaps, directed by the supervisor, wherein the consequences of failure to meet expectations have been clearly spelled out *in advance.* Then, of course, objective measurement of actual performance can provide the information necessary to determine what, if any, disciplinary action is indicated.

The use of performance appraisal for *development* purposes, however, is altogether different. Here we concentrate primarily on the future—not just for promotional considerations but rather for what is required to make the individual a more effective employee. Furthermore, there is a distinct reversal of roles on the part of the supervisor who must now function more as a *counselor* than in the *judge* role, which is predominant in each of the other applications. Actually, in looking at performance appraisal as a *development* tool, it is far more important to properly determine what should be done during the next report period than it is to examine what was done during the previous one. This is not as incongruous as it may seem. The real key to effective use of objectives and results for employee development purposes lies in its motivational impact. The mutual involvement of the employee and his or her immediate supervisor in the setting of meaningful growth objectives is the most significant step in the process.

Please recognize that performance appraisal used for development purposes and the resultant higher performance expectations from employees is the *only* application that has high "value added" benefit for *all three* affected groups—the organization, the supervisor, and the individual employee. It is this recognition that must become readily apparent to all those affected if they are to be motivated to do more than merely comply with job requirements. Furthermore, it is this recognition that must bring about the realization of the need to *separate in time* those performance appraisals done for development purposes from those done to satisfy other needs. Not only must they be separate in time, appraisals for development purposes must *precede* the others to have any real meaning.

The real difference, subtle as it may be, is that, properly administered, appraisals conducted for such purposes as salary review, promotability, layoffs, reassignment, disciplinary action, etc., will be easier, more effective, and more reliable if they have been preceded in time, three months or more, by an appraisal for development purposes. In other words, periodic performance appraisals for development should be conducted at times when we are *not* concerned with decisions about salaries, promotions, layoffs, reassignments, or possible disciplinary action. We can then concentrate on the satisfaction of development needs as the principal outcome of our appraisals. (Ironically, if we do our job of appraisal properly at that time, we have a much more useful data base for making those later critical decisions on salaries, etc.)

We will address both sets of applications in this book; however, we will place greater emphasis on the *development* role since, properly handled, it will require a heavier investment of both the supervisor's and the employee's time and will provide the highest potential "payoff" on that investment.

The Need for Joint Action and Commitment.   Traditionally, the approach in performance appraisal has been one in which the supervisor tells the employee what to do, supervises the doing of it, and then, theoretically, provides feedback on how well it was done. Douglas McGregor first called attention to the inherent problems in this approach in his classic 1957 *Harvard Business Review* article.[5] He later made some observations on companies and supervisors that had been successful in introducing changes in approach. These changes were from the traditional one-sided approach "to one based on *joint* planning and goal setting, helping the subordinate achieve goals that he has been actively involved in establishing, and later joint evaluation of how well the goals have been achieved, with primary emphasis on the subordinate's self-evaluation.

> Some companies failed to see the fundamental differences between the two approaches. They made certain superficial changes in procedure without altering a style that was much like the first of the two described above; thus, they adapted to their own situation. New personnel forms, a new label ("management by objectives"), and new tactics were introduced, but that was all.
>
> These companies have generally been dissatisfied with the results of their efforts. Many of them have concluded that the ideas proposed . . . were idealistic, impractical, or just plain wrong.[6]

This is the essence of what is probably the most critical change from tradition that is required. Those organizations that are using the label "management by objectives" in this sense are the ones that cause it to be called just another fad or gimmick rather than the professional approach to management that it really is.

The whole concept of Management by Objectives and Results (MOR) is built on the principles of *joint* action and commitment on the part of both the supervisor and the employee. Without that, it becomes just another device for getting the employee to do what the supervisor wants done. As such, it will soon be discarded as ineffective, either through apathy or through open resistance. (See Chapter 3 for a description of MOR principles and techniques.)

McGregor amplified further on the importance of a sense of commitment: *"Human response to information about performance varies with commitment to goals.* The purpose of any information feedback control loop is to achieve some standards of performance."[7] Herein lies the real strength of the approach to performance appraisals that we are advocating. *With a true commitment to specific goals on the part of the employee, the appraisal and development process is largely self-administering.* No supervisor, regardless of how forceful or inspiring she or he may be, can be as effective a taskmaster as a properly motivated individual. If that individual truly believes in a development program that is *self*-established (with the supervisor's concurrence), he or she will keep personal track of that performance with the supervisor serving primarily as "conscience" and counselor.

There is one other vital area in which joint action is required, and that is in achieving a compatibility between individual goals and organizational goals. Levinson once again zeros in on what can be a major flaw in using management by objectives in the appraisal process if steps are not taken to overcome it:

> If a man's [sic] most powerful driving force is comprised of his needs, wishes, and personal aspirations, combined with the compelling wish to look good in his own eyes for meeting those deeply held personal goals, then management by objectives should begin with *his* objectives. What does he want to do with his life? Where does he want to go? What will make him feel good about himself? What does he want to be able to look back on when he has expended his unrecoverable years?[8]

Levinson lends direction to his thesis by pointing out that "the fundamental managerial consideration necessarily must be focused on the question: 'How do we meet both individual and organizational purposes?' If a major intention of management by objectives is to enlist the self-motivated commitment of the individual, then that commitment must derive from the individual's powerful wishes to support the organization's goals; otherwise the commitment will be merely identical to his personal wishes."[9]

This, then, more than ever identifies the importance of the counseling role to be played by the supervisor. If the supervisor can assist the employees in clarifying personal goals and establishing their relationship with the goals of the organization, that will be a major contribution. Even if it is determined that the two sets of goals are not completely compatible, having them out in the open where they can be examined critically will be mutually beneficial.

Some of these departures from tradition will not be particularly earth-shaking to many supervisors who have already looked for innovative approaches to making the appraisal process work for them. For a truly effective approach to performance appraisal, however, all of these departures must be integrated into it. The supervisor who has already taken all of these factors into consideration probably does not need to read any further in this book.

SUMMARY

Performance appraisal, properly used, is one of the most powerful supervisory tools available. The fact that it is not meeting its potential in many organizations is no secret, particularly to those in middle- and first-line supervision who have the greatest responsibility for its effective use. A change for the better in the use of this valuable tool will require a conscious departure from certain traditional practices, specifically: (1) the use of objective more than subjective forms of measurement together with concentration on performance rather than personality; (2) the use of a tailored rather than a standard approach; (3) the separation of performance appraisal for development purposes from the multipurpose evaluation; and (4) the need for *joint* action and commitment on the part of both the supervisor and the employee.

The philosophy and techniques applied in the process known as Management by Objectives and Results (MOR) are especially useful in any meaningful performance appraisal effort. They incorporate what is perhaps the most effective means of integrating the necessary departures from traditional practices into an approach that is both dynamic and functional. Furthermore, even though we see the appraisal process having its greatest value in relation to employee development, the use of objectives and results in this context also can provide the kind of data necessary for making meaningful decisions on such matters as salary, promotion, layoff, reassignment, or disciplinary action, together with the needed documentation to support those decisions.

ENDNOTES

1. Robert I. Lazer and Walter S. Wikstrom, *Appraising Managerial Performance: Current Practices and Future Directions* (New York: The Conference Board, Inc., 1977).
2. Ibid., pp. 22–23.

3. Reprinted by permission of the *Harvard Business Review*. Excerpt from "Management By Whose Objectives?" by Harry Levinson (July–August 1970). Copyright © 1970 by the President and Fellows of Harvard College; all rights reserved.
4. Lazer and Wikstrom, *Appraising Managerial Performance,* p. 17.
5. Douglas McGregor, "An Uneasy Look at Performance Appraisal," *The Harvard Business Review* (May–June 1957): 89–94.
6. Douglas McGregor, *The Professional Manager* (New York: McGraw-Hill Book Company, 1967).
7. Ibid., p. 125.
8. Levinson, "Management By Whose Objectives?" p. 129.
9. Ibid., p. 132.

2

Performance Appraisals—Issues and Concerns

This book has been prepared in two editions—this one directed at *Business and Industry* and another one for *Public Sector* organizations. While every organization tends to feel that its circumstances are unique, my experience in working with several organizations in both the public and private sectors is that the differences between the two are far more in degree than they are in kind. In this chapter, we will draw some parallels between what is happening in governmental organizations today and some of the issues and concerns related to the use of performance appraisals in business and industrial companies.

It is an accepted premise that the use of performance appraisal in many, if not most, organizations in both the public and private sectors has been perfunctory at best. While there have been some companies and some units within companies who have worked hard at improving their effectiveness in the use of this important management tool, by and large, most managers will readily admit that they have not put any more effort into the appraisal process than was absolutely necessary to meet the paperwork requirements of the job.

The one significant recent development in government that does not have a parallel in the private sector was the introduction of the Civil Service Reform Act (CSRA), which put managers in the federal government on notice that considerably more was going to be expected in the future. Needless to say, the reaction of managers affected has run the full gamut from "it's about time!" to "just another bureaucratic paperwork exercise." While we are not likely to have such sweeping legislation universally affecting private sector companies, such legislation as Equal Employment Opportunity, Affirmative Action, Flexible Age Retirement, and disclosure laws have certainly had, and will continue to have, impact in that sector as well.

SPECIAL ISSUES AND CONCERNS RELATED TO THE USE OF PERFORMANCE APPRAISALS

Aside from all the benefits identified in Chapter 1, there are some specific issues and concerns related to the use of performance appraisals. Some of these have more relevance in governmental organizations, such as "Prop. 13 Fever"—the taxpayers' revolt, Civil Service—limitations and new developments, and relation to legislative bodies, which we have addressed specifically in the *Public Sector* version. However, there are some issues and concerns that have similar, if not equal, relevance in the private sector, plus some that are unique to business and industry. Let me cite, and then elaborate on, some of those that are most frequently identified:

> Role of the Personnel, Industrial Relations, or Human Resources Department
>
> Relation to Unions
>
> Documentation Requirements
>
> Performance Appraisals in Matrix Organizations
>
> Relation to Parent Companies
>
> The Effect of the "Baby Boom"

I will offer some comments and suggestions on each of these issues and concerns, but be prepared for a high degree of ambiguity in some of my responses. In most cases, there are no straightforward "how-to-do-it" solutions. As supervisors, however, you must learn to cope with them.

Role of the Personnel, Industrial Relations, or Human Resources Department

The Problem

In most business and industrial companies of reasonable size (1,000 employees or more), the administration of a performance appraisal system falls under the purview of the staff department that has the responsibility for what has been called traditionally the Personnel function. This "administration" could include any or all of the following activities: designing and/or distributing appraisal forms, preparing guidelines or manuals for their use, conducting orientation or training sessions related to performance appraisal, receiving and retaining official appraisal records, coaching or counseling individual supervisors and employees on appraisal-related matters, advising top management on performance appraisal policy, and analyzing results for effective organizational impact and usage. If performance appraisal is the "key to effective supervision" (as stated in the subtitle to this book), why is the Personnel Department so heavily involved? Is this really a management tool or another "Personnel program"?

Response

Having something seen as "another Personnel program" is relegating it to an exercise in futility, in my judgment. Yet, unfortunately, that is exactly the view that many supervisors have of the performance appraisal process. Part of this is due to an overzealous effort on the part of some people in some Personnel Departments. Part of it is because performance appraisal is a responsibility that many supervisors would prefer not having and the Personnel Department becomes an easy scapegoat.

The reality of life is that, unless there were some staff organization, like the Personnel Department, playing a forcing role, the likelihood of performance appraisals taking place in more than a small minority of cases in most companies is virtually nonexistent. One of the legitimate functions of such an organization is to be the company "conscience"—getting supervisors to do what they should have been doing anyway. The mutual understanding between a supervisor and an employee on what constitutes satisfactory performance, i.e., performance standards and/or objectives, should be an essential part of supervisory responsibility. The effective use of a performance appraisal system can be one of the most valuable tools available to the supervisor. Given the fact that measurable criteria have been spelled out in advance (hopefully by mutual agreement), measurement of performance against them becomes almost self-evident. The supervisor is in a much stronger position, then, to support any related personnel decisions.

Personnel specialists frequently have the expertise necessary to increase the probability of well-designed performance appraisal systems that will encourage fair and consistent application throughout the company. This is especially important when it comes to such matters as merit pay, promotions, and adverse actions related to individual employees. Inconsistency or apparent lack of fairness in these areas are where a company and a supervisor may be especially vulnerable. It is a role of the Personnel Department to reduce that vulnerability. Regardless of the level of the affected employee, the use of performance elements, standards, and objectives cannot help but make the supervisor's job more productive and more defensible when it comes to making and supporting personnel decisions, whether related to adverse action or merit pay.

The major concern I have with this discussion is that the emphasis is still too heavily on the *negative* and *scorekeeping* aspects of the process. The primary thesis of this book is that, although that may be the most visible and the most discussed aspect of the performance appraisal process, it is a long way from being its most important. The supervisor who can make use of performance appraisal as a major management tool to improve the overall effectiveness of his or her unit and its employees will be the one who is getting the best return on the investment of time and effort in the process. Presumably, that supervisor will also benefit from higher personal performance ratings since helping her or his employees to become more effective should be the most, or at least one of the most, important performance elements for that supervisor.

Relation to Unions

The Problem

There are many companies whose employees are covered under some sort of a collective bargaining agreement with one or more recognized labor organizations or unions. Although it varies depending on the local agreement, most such employees are not excluded from the performance appraisal process because of their bargaining unit status. This introduces the participation of a third party in discussions related to performance standards. How can a supervisor do a conscientious job of developing performance standards when the union gets in the way?

Response

First of all, not all union representatives are obstructionists. There are many who are just as concerned about producing quality products and services as any member of management. Their job, and rightfully so under the terms of the contract, is to make certain that employees are not exploited in the process. Under most collective bargaining agreements, it is management's right to establish reasonable standards of performance for its employees. By and large, the substance of the performance elements and standards are not negotiable, provided they do not discriminate against an individual or group of employees. Generally, in a bargaining unit agreement, the supervisor must write the standards to be applied. Whether or not union representatives and/or employees participate in their determination will depend on the agreement. In most cases, the standards arrived at must be communicated to the union before they are given to employees. You should check the provisions of your own agreement before proceeding. The truly successful supervisor is one who views the union representative not as an adversary but as another member of the team with whom an understanding must be reached. "Union relations" may well be a key result area or performance element for a supervisor in a bargaining unit for which a performance standard or objective may be in order.

Documentation Requirements

The Problem

Failure to adequately document the justification for certain personnel actions, favorable as well as unfavorable, has come back to haunt many managers in both the private and public sectors. There have been many federal and local laws passed in recent years that makes documentation of various personnel actions mandatory. Some even carry the spectre of possible civil and/or criminal liability. How can the poor supervisor keep up with the paperwork jungle and still get the job done?

Response

Proper documentation for personnel actions has been a requirement in most organizations for many years. Recent legislation and related litigation has merely served to reemphasize that need. (See Morris Bryson's article, "Documentation—Its Importance in Performance Appraisal," in the Appendix for a further elaboration on the subject.) My observation is that many supervisors spend an inordinate amount of energy "fighting the system" emotionally. This usually results in an excessive amount of frustration, a less than completely satisfactory job of documentation, and the expenditure of far more actual time on the task than is necessary. My recommendation, as emotionally unsatisfying as it may be, is to accept the fact that it must be done (stop fighting it), get the necessary knowledge and skill to do the job satisfactorily (your Personnel, Industrial Relations, or Human Resources Department can help you), and get it done as quickly as possible (so it won't be hanging over your head). Honestly, it is not as difficult as it seems, and the more often you do it correctly, the easier it becomes.

Performance Appraisals in Matrix Organizations

The Problem

More and more companies, particularly in high technology, are functioning under some form of matrix management. While there are many variations of matrix management, typically an employee such as an engineer or a physicist would report to a functional supervisor for administrative purposes and to one or more program or project managers for technical direction. The relationship with the supervisor is a continuing one, while the relationship with the program manager is likely to be transient depending on the particular need for that employee's services. In effect, the supervisor is managing a "job shop" whereby employees are placed on specific projects only as long as their expertise is needed. Then they are shifted to other projects requiring their services. It is generally conceded to be the most efficient way to make use of human talent that is in limited supply and is frequently high priced. It often does create other problems, however. The program manager may end up competing with other program managers for the use of the same talent at the same time. The supervisor, who normally has the responsibility for appraising the performance of the employee, may have little direct knowledge of the employee's performance and, in fact, may not be technically competent to make such an evaluation. How can you be held accountable for performance appraisals when you have little or no direct supervision of the employee's work?

Response

There have been several things written on matrix management that go into much more depth than we can here. While there are many inherent organizational problems with it, not the least of which is the effective use of performance appraisal, I do not know of any project-oriented organization that can survive without some form of matrix management. The cost of operating any other way is prohibitive. Therefore, it means that supervisors within such organizations must learn to adapt to the complexities of a matrix relationship if they intend to be effective in their supervisory roles.

While there are some things, such as team-building efforts involving both program managers and supervisors, that can help improve the overall communications in such organizations, some specific techniques will be addressed here for making the performance appraisal process more effective. The key, of course, is frequent and open communication between the supervisor, the program manager, and the affected employee. Some specific ideas include:

1. Clear written statements of work are essential at the outset. These need to be modified periodically to bring them in line with current effort.

2. Regularly scheduled progress reviews (at least quarterly, preferably monthly) between the supervisor and employee are necessary to keep the supervisor current and to make any modifications in the performance appraisal agreement that may be appropriate.

3. Performance appraisal discussions (advance agreement, progress reviews, evaluation) might involve all three parties (supervisor, program manager, employee), particularly if the employee's work is primarily related to one program manager, with the supervisor having the final accountability.

4. Separate discussions between the supervisor and the program manager may be appropriate prior to formal discussions with the employee.

5. Periodic *scheduled* reviews are strongly recommended between the supervisor and the various program managers served to discuss employee progress plus any work changes. (This could cover more than one employee, if appropriate.)

6. Written summaries of performance by program managers about specific employees can and should be included in the performance appraisal process.

7. A department policy requiring both supervisors and program managers to have one or more objectives related to matrix communications and performance appraisals may be desirable. (For example, "To reach agreement with each program manager we serve by (date) on performance appraisals for each related employee at a cost not to exceed two hours of my time per employee.)"

Relation to Parent Companies

The Problem

Mergers and acquisitions have drawn a lot of attention in recent years. Many companies, both large and small, have been and are being faced with a need to make some fairly radical changes in the way they function. Some such "marriages" are "friendly," and desired by all related parties, while others take place in an extremely hostile atmosphere. Some resultant parent companies play largely a holding company role with relatively little involvement with member companies other than a demand to "send money," whereas others tend to make sweeping changes and get deeply involved in the day-to-day management decisions. Some have a management philosophy that is highly compatible with that of member companies; others come from a substantially different point of view. Local personnel policies may remain the same or they may have to be brought in conformity with that of the parent company. How can you implement any kind of a meaningful performance appraisal system when someone in another company can change signals on you at any time?

Response

There is a strong indication that the current trend toward mergers and acquisitions will continue and may even escalate over the next decade. There are several economists that are predicting a much heavier concentration of business activity in a small number of large conglomerates. In fact, one of the opportunities that many entrepreneurs seek is to build a company to the point where it is attractive to another company with a resultant sale of stock or improvement of equity at a substantial rate. Therefore, any supervisor in a solid company should anticipate and perhaps even look forward to the possibility of that company becoming a part of a larger organization.

At any rate, my observation has been that very few parent companies will interfere significantly with a member company's performance appraisal system if it is producing meaningful results. Therefore, as with any approach to management, your best defense is a good offense. If you have a working system that is achieving the kind of employee appraisal and development results that are worthwhile, you are in an excellent position to maintain and build on it. Forms may change and there may be some different emphasis, but no achievement-oriented parent company is going to tamper with a system that is producing results.

The Effect of the "Baby Boom"

The Problem

In the late 1940s and early 1950s there was an unprecedented increase in the birth rate in the United States and many other countries. It has come to be known as the post-World War II "baby boom." It continued for several years with a moderate reversal of birth rate trends in the 1960s and 1970s, brought about by increases in the divorce rate and two-career families, as well as more widespread use of birth control methods. The resultant impact on the work force over the next decade or so is an extraordinarily heavy concentration of employees in their mid thirties to late forties, with decreasing percentages of people in their twenties and early thirties. Since the period from about age thirty-five to age fifty is the time in many people's careers when they expect to make their moves into middle and higher level management, there is a strong likelihood that the number of qualified candidates for senior management positions is going to exceed by far the number of available spots. This means that many highly capable people will have "topped out" in their careers at a somewhat earlier age than was common in the past. What is the point in developing yourself and in helping others develop themselves when there is nowhere to go?

Response

There is no question but that the "baby boom crunch" is going to be one of the critical human issues facing management in the immediate future. On the one hand, it means that people ultimately selected for senior positions are likely to be better qualified than has been true in the past, if for no other reason than there will be a larger pool of candidates to draw from. The downside risk here is that the pent up frustration that is likely to exist in people who are stymied in their career advancement plans may not be readily visible, and management decision makers may not be sensitive to the potentially festering sore that could be developing in an otherwise highly productive organization. My response here will be addressed first to the individual and then to corporate management and, more specifically, the supervisor.

For the individual, it becomes more important than ever to decide what direction is both realistic and desirable in terms of your own future career. There will probably be more opportunities for advancement into senior management positions in the future than there were in the past. The problem is that the competition for these positions will be much greater than it used to be. Consequently, the sacrifices an individual will be called on to make in terms of education (formal and informal), personal time invested, specific job assignments, possible geographical moves, etc., could be substantial. You must decide if you are willing to make the personal investment in that type of a career direction that will require virtually a full scale commitment. The days of being selected for a career advancing position by virtue of being in the right place at the right time are rapidly diminishing. The key to your own emotional well being is that *you must make a decision* one way or the other. Failure to make that decision with the vague hope that something favorable will happen, even though you have not made the personal commitment to action, is a sure trip to frustration and low self-esteem.

If your decision is that you are not willing or able to make the personal commitment to a senior management career path, then accept that as an "OK" decision. You can still resolve to continually work toward becoming more effective in your current position, perhaps expanding into other related fields which, presumably, will result in increasing your relative value to your employer. There are opportunities for satisfying your need for recognition and self-fulfillment in nonjob-related endeavors such as sports and recreational pursuits, hobbies and self-improvement activities, personal and family relationships, and service relationships. (See my book, *Getting Your Act Together: Goal Setting for Fun, Health and Profit,* for additional ideas in this regard.)

If your decision is that you are willing and able to make the kind of commitment necessary to pursue a career in senior management, then you can use the performance appraisal process as a vehicle to help move you along that path. It will become more and more a case of both careful preparation on your part plus regular communication inquiring into and reinforcing your interest in such a career direction. Specific suggestions include:

1. Identify the kinds of senior management positions (in other companies as well as your own) that would be appealing to you and that would represent a reasonable career direction for you. Avoid focusing on a single position, at least at the outset, to keep your options open.

2. Learn as much as you can about what people in such positions do and what they did to prepare themselves for that responsibility. There are many books and periodicals containing valuable insights. Your public library can be a tremendous resource.

3. Interview people in other companies as well as your own who occupy positions similar to the ones that interest you. Ironically, most such people are extremely flattered to share their insights and experience *provided* you make it clear that you are seeking career advice and counsel, not a job.

4. Chart a tentative career plan for yourself, including the kinds of work experience and specific education and training you might need. Seek advice from others if it is not clear from your research already.

5. Make your current supervisor and, as appropriate, others in your company aware of your career interests when you have made your decision, if you have not already involved them in your initial discussions. Do not assume they will automatically recognize your potential.

6. As appropriate, ask that your career interests and your plan for moving in that direction be included as a part of your performance appraisal in addition to whatever may be directed at your current position. Seek, rather than wait for, periodic reviews of your progress as a further means of reinforcing your interest.

Both corporate management and the individual supervisor can use the performance appraisal process as a means of addressing the "baby boom" issue *before* it becomes a major source of employee frustration. The Personnel, Industrial Relations, or Human Resources Department can play a significant role in helping this take place. Specific suggestions include:

1. Assess the current employee population to determine the proportion that fall into the "baby boom" category, including a projection of the percentage of that group likely to consider themselves (realistically or not) as having senior management potential.

2. Make a projection (optimistic, pessimistic, and most likely) of the number and kinds of senior management positions becoming available over the next five to ten years.

3. Encourage and assist affected employees in exploring the various career paths open to them both inside and outside the company.

4. Incorporate as a part of the performance appraisal process a frank discussion of the management career opportunities and limitations, including the joint (supervisor and employee) establishment of developmental plans appropriate to the individual employee.

5. Provide and/or encourage opportunities for employees with capabilities, current or potential, to make use of these capabilities in nonjob-related endeavors such as professional societies, community service organizations, company-sponsored recreational and special interest groups, etc. As appropriate, provide reasonable company time and expense reimbursement in connection with these pursuits. (This modest investment could pay rich dividends in retaining the loyalty and dedication of capable employees whose advancement in the company may be limited.)

The degree of impact from the "baby boom crunch" will vary widely among companies, but virtually every company of reasonable size (1,000 or more employees) will be affected. Those that anticipate this and use the performance appraisal process accordingly will be stronger as a result.

SUMMARY

Performance appraisal has a legitimate place in business and industry and in governmental organizations as well. As taxpayers, I believe that most of us would agree that we have a right to know that tax dollars are being spent judiciously, that governmental employees are being held accountable for performing their jobs satisfactorily, and that those same employees are being given the opportunity to grow and become even more valuable (and that they will be suitably recognized for that). While the related consequences may not be as visible nor as controversial in business and industry, most rational people would accept the same purposes as being equally valid in the private sector. The effective use of the performance appraisal process is essential to serving those purposes.

That there are some significant differences in the way performance appraisals must be handled in both the private and public sectors is obvious. The same kinds of differences might be cited when comparing an engineering organization to a sales organization to a manufacturing organization to a service organization. However, most of these differences are far more in degree than in kind. Since some form of performance appraisal is an accepted practice in most organizations, a supervisor may choose to ignore it, fight it, or try to beat it. The truly successful supervisor, however, will look on such a system as a vehicle for strengthening the contributions to be made by the people in his or her unit, accepting and, when necessary, compensating for whatever limitations and restrictions may affect that system. By looking for what is *right* with the system, rather than what is wrong with it, that supervisor can put it to work for the benefit of all concerned.

3

MOR Revisited*

Since our approach to performance appraisal is based largely on the concepts and techniques in *Management by Objectives and Results for Business and Industry,* let's reexamine briefly the total MOR process in general, then look specifically at those steps that have the greatest bearing on the performance appraisal and development process, as it affects managers in business and industry. It is not essential, of course, that an organization be fully committed to the MOR approach for a manager to apply the principles and techniques of performance appraisal and development discussed in this text; however, a general understanding of its philosophy and methodology is necessary.

MOR—AN OVERVIEW

Management by Objectives and Results (MOR) is a common-sense, systematic approach to getting things done that is based on principles and techniques that many good managers have been practicing for decades. In spite of the new jargon that has come into vogue, there is nothing mysterious about it. It does not require a manager to stop what he or she has been doing successfully for years and learn a whole new approach. That would be idiotic. It does require the manager to focus on *results* rather than activities, building on the strengths that she or he has developed over the years with modifications and additions as good judgment dictates. Its effect should be in reducing the "fire fighting" syndrome (it can never be completely eliminated) with greater attention being given to "fire prevention" as the mark of a truly professional manager.

The MOR process is deceptively simple. Most managers and students of management do not have great difficulty in comprehending it intellectually. After all, it is perfectly logical. The difficulty comes in application because it

---

*Adapted from George L. Morrisey, *Management by Objectives for Business and Industry,* Addison-Wesley Publishing Co., Reading, Massachusetts, 1977.

does require systematic planning—an uncomfortable activity for many of us. It can be illustrated graphically as a horizontal funnel (Fig. 3.1). As a process, it moves from the general to the specific. Its purpose is to subdivide an effort that is large and complex until it reaches a unit size that is manageable. Then it is integrated through a human process that promotes understanding, involvement, and commitment.

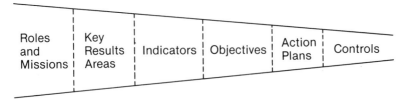

Fig. 3.1 Six steps in the MOR funnel.

Roles and Missions describe the nature and scope of the work to be performed. They establish the reason for the organization's existence. The "organization" can be the entire enterprise or the specific organizational unit(s) for which this particular manager is accountable. A description of the economic, functional, and other commitments involved, plus a determination of the philosophical basis for conducting the organization's affairs, are an integral part of this step in the MOR process. Once established, it is not likely to change unless there is a significant change in what the organization will be doing.

Key Results Areas relate to the job of the individual manager or specialist. (These can be equated with Performance Elements, Key Responsibilities, Critical Factors, and other similar labels.) Unless it is a one-person organization, factors identified here will have some significant differences as well as some similarities with those identified under Roles and Missions. They fix priority on where the time, energy, and talent of the individual manager or specialist should be concentrated. Examples of Key Results Areas are Productivity, Cost Control, Personal Production, Unit Production, Workforce Utilization, Customer/Client Relations, Staff Development, and Self Development. They normally are limited to five to ten for each individual, so that the "critical few" rather than the "trivial many" can be concentrated on.

Indicators are those factors, capable of being measured, that can be looked at within each Key Results Area to give an indication of effective or ineffective performance. (These can be equated with the measurable portion of typical performance standards.) Clearly, these are not absolute measurements (there are none in management), and they can be manipulated with relative ease. (I have yet to see a management system that I couldn't "beat" if I set my mind to it.) In order for the Indicators to work, the individual and her or his supervisor must agree that the Indicators selected will provide reasonable visibility of performance. Furthermore, there must be an assumption of integrity on the part of all concerned. An example of an Indicator of Productivity is output per work-hour; of Staff Development, the number of employees with a mutually agreed on and implemented development plan. Note that the Indicators identify only *what* will be measured, not how much or in what direction. They serve as an intermediate step, prior to setting objectives (or performance standards), designed to increase the probability that we are directing the use of our resources to where they will get the best payoff.

Objectives are statements of measurable results to be achieved. Generally, they will relate to one or more of the individual's Key Results Areas and Indicators. They can be clearly expressed according to this model: To (action or accomplishment verb) (single key result) by (target date) at (cost). For example, "To increase output per work-hour by 10 percent, without loss of quality, effective January 1, at an implementation cost not to exceed $5,000 and one hundred work-hours"; or "To reach agreement on and begin implementation of an individual development plan with not less than four of my immediate employees within First Quarter at a cost not to exceed current budget and forty hours of my time." Using a Performance Standards approach to measurement, these same objectives could be stated as follows:

Key results areas	Acceptable	Superior	Excellent
Productivity	Same output per work-hour as last year	10% increase	15% + increase
Staff Development	Implemented dev. plans with two employees	Implemented dev. plans with four employees	Implemented dev. plans with all employees

Action Plans are the sequence of actions to be carried out in order to achieve the objective. An Action Plan incorporates the substeps of programming, scheduling, budgeting, and fixing accountability, plus reviewing and reconciling. It is the part of the MOR process that describes how the objective will be achieved, by when, and at what cost; it also fixes accountability for completion of each piece of action. This helps establish a hierarchy of objectives in that many action steps will become objectives for lower level employees. Action plans are broken down only to that amount of detail required for the accountable manager to make his or her contribution to the objective. The responsibility for determining further detail should rest on the shoulders of the individual performing the action.

Controls are designed to keep the accountable manager informed of progress against objectives. They close the loop in the MOR process and provide the rationale for adding the phrase "and Results" to "Management by Objectives. . . ." Objectives, by themselves, are meaningless unless there is some way of ensuring their accomplishment. To the extent possible, they should be visual (I favor simple charts) and should provide for adequate visibility in a timely fashion (sufficient to take corrective action if required) with the least expenditure of time and effort.

Communication is the catalyst that ties the whole process together. MOR is not a mechanical system, it is a human one. The process must serve as a communication vehicle among the people affected. As people become *involved* in the decisions that affect them, they become *committed* to carrying them out. That is where the real payoff comes.

MOR AND PERFORMANCE APPRAISAL

In Chapter 1, we identified three discrete skills necessary for a supervisor to function effectively in the area of performance appraisal: developing performance measurement criteria, interpersonal communications, and documentation. MOR is especially useful as it relates to the first and third of these. It is also useful in interpersonal communications in that it provides a more rational basis for discussion, even though it does not address communication skills per se.

As far as the development of performance measurement criteria and documentation are concerned, the three steps in the MOR process that are most useful are Key Results Areas, Indicators, and Objectives. While all of the other steps make a contribution, these three provide the specific data that will make an effective performance appraisal possible. Let's review each of these in more detail.

Determining Key Results Areas

Key Results Areas help determine where the individual manager or specialist should be investing her or his time, energy, and talents. *Key* Results Areas are just that. They do not cover everything an individual does; such a list would be unmanageable. They identify those areas where *results,* not activities, are significant enough to warrant specific attention. There are many things an individual does in the course of the daily routine that will happen, regardless of whether or not objectives are established for them. There are others which, in all probability, could be reduced in intensity, delegated, or eliminated altogether.

Guidelines for Determining Key Results Areas
There are nine basic guidelines that, under normal circumstances, will help an individual determine his or her key results areas.

1. They will identify all major areas within which the accountable individual will be expected to invest time, energy, talent, and other resources during the projected time period of commitment (usually six months to one year).

2. They will include both managerial and operational responsibilities of the accountable individual.

3. They will cover both normal work output expectations and innovations or improvement efforts.

4. They will include "soft" or difficult-to-measure areas, such as Staff Development, Organizational Relationships, and Public Relations, as well as "hard" tangible areas that are easier to measure, such as Personal Production, Unit Production, and Cost Control.

5. They will not necessarily cover the entire job, but will instead identify the "critical few" areas in which priority effort should be directed.

6. Each will be limited, generally, to one, two, or three words.

7. They will not represent activities as such, but rather areas within which activities and, more importantly, *results* will occur.

8. Each will not be measurable as stated, but will contain elements that are capable of being made measurable.

9. Collectively, they will form a basis for effective communication up, down, and across organizational lines.

Sample Key Results Areas

This is a list of frequently used key results areas, some of which would be useful in many jobs. Many of these, of course, would not be appropriate for a given individual's job, and there are others, not identified here, that would be more pertinent. Use this list as a guide, not a prescription.

Common to all managers

Staff Development

Staff Morale

Organizational Relationships

Social Responsibilities

Personal Production (be specific)

Personal Staff Assistance to Management

Self Development

Anticipation/Innovation

Common to many managers

Strategic Planning

Operational Planning

Unit Production

Productivity

Workforce Utilization

Quality Control

Cost Control

Unit Administration

Corporate Relations

Public Relations

Management Communications

Organizational Image

Client/User Contacts

Product or Service Design

Legal Responsibilities

Contract Negotiations

Identifying and Specifying Indicators of Effectiveness

Indicators are those measurable factors within a given key results area on which it is worthwhile to set objectives or performance standards. They identify only *what* will be measured, not how much or by when (that comes in the objective or standard). They may represent "hard" numbers, such as units of production per work-hour or number of clients served. They could be problems that need to be overcome, for example, interpreting product changes to customers or eliminating a backlog of work. Or they could be "soft" numbers indicating effectiveness in *subjective* key results areas, such as turnover of personnel or absenteeism as indicators of Staff Morale, or number of complaints or requests for service as indicators of Client/User Satisfaction.

It is possible, of course, to leap immediately from agreed-upon key results areas to objectives or performance standards without going through the indicator step. In those instances where the objective or standard is obvious, by all means go directly to it. Only use the indicator step where the objective or standard is *not* clear or where there may be several different ways of measuring the same thing.

Guidelines for Identifying and Specifying Indicators

Under normal circumstances, a manager's indicators will meet the following criteria:

1. They are measurable factors, falling logically with a given key results area, on which objectives may be set.

2. They may represent:
    a. "Hard" numbers, e.g., units of production per work-hour or number of clients served;
    b. *Problems* to be overcome, e.g., interpreting changes in the law to constituents or eliminating a backlog of work; or
    c. "Soft" numbers or indicators of effectiveness in subjective areas, e.g., turnover of personnel or absenteeism related to Staff Morale.

3. They usually identify only *what* will be measured, not how much or in what direction, for example, rework as a percentage of total effort, not 10 percent reduction in rework. Indicators only identify where effort should be focused.

4. They will fall, principally, into one of the following time dimensions, in descending order of usefulness:
    a. *Concurrent* indicators—factors that can be identified in advance and tracked during performance against objectives, e.g., output per work-hour;

b. *Pre*indicators—factors identified *before* the fact that will point toward a course of action, e.g., economic trends, election year impact; or

c. *Terminal* indicators—factors that can be measured only after the fact, e.g., project completion, number of promotions.

5. The cost of identifying and monitoring them will not exceed the value of the information.

Sample Indicators

The following is a list of frequently used indicators related to typical key results areas for managers in many organizations. These indicators are designed only to stimulate your own thinking, since there are many others that might serve as well or better for you in your situation.

Productivity

Output per work-hour	Down time
Output per individual	Turnaround time
Schedule maintenance	Problems overcome

Operational planning

MOR application	Resource determination
Staff loading	Control checks
Work flow plan	

Financial results

Actual/budget	Cash flow
Cost per unit output	Return on assets
Net profit on sales	Margin per unit

Strategic planning

Long-range plan	Facility development plan
Market research completed	Human resource projections
Product phase-out plan	

Staff development

Training participation	Cross-training plan
Number of promotions	Number of employees with development plan
MOR use by staff	

Staff morale

Personnel turnover	Number of new ideas
Absenteeism	Voluntary participation
Number of grievances	

Selecting and Setting Objectives (Performance Standards)

The setting of objectives is the most obvious step in the process we call Management by Objectives and Results. In fact, this step can be used independently of the rest of the process when it is desirable to do so. It is particularly useful in planning special projects, meetings, business trips, personal pursuits—anything for which it is important to focus on the results to be achieved. Objectives form the basis for determining what activities should be performed and also help establish criteria for evaluating how well they are being performed. Therefore, the setting of objectives is one of the keys to effective management.

An objective is a statement of results to be achieved. Such a statement contains four major elements: (1) an action or accomplishment verb, (2) a single measurable key result, (3) a date or time period within which the result is to be accomplished, and (4) the maximum investment, in terms of money, work-hours, or both, we are willing to make toward its accomplishment. An objective follows the model: To (action or accomplishment verb) (single key result) by (target date) at (cost). For example, "To reduce by 10 percent the cost of Operation A by January 1 at an implementation cost not to exceed 50 work-hours" or "To develop and implement a new work flow plan for the unit effective March 1 at a cost not to exceed 60 work-hours" or "To achieve a minimum of 95 percent on-time delivery of all standard orders each month starting in March at an implementation cost not to exceed $5,000 out-of-pocket and 200 work-hours."

Note that these objectives do not include a justification for their existence nor a description of how they should be accomplished. An objective identifies only the *what, when,* and *how much.* The "why" comes before, and the "how" comes afterward.

How Do Objectives Relate to "Performance Standards"?

While many objectives can be stated as performance standards, and vice versa, I see them as serving different purposes in the performance appraisal process. The most effective performance appraisal document probably should contain some of both. (While some performance appraisal policies specify the use of "performance standards" without mention of "objectives," there is nothing in most such plans that precludes the use of both; therefore there is room for adaptation, as appropriate.) I see a "performance standard" as the achievement and/or maintenance of a level of performance in ongoing efforts such as quality, productivity, cost control, etc. It would be possible to develop a set of performance standards that might be generic to people in comparable positions (such as regional or district sales managers). On the other hand, I see "objectives" as accomplishments that may or may not be of an ongoing nature. They could be related to overcoming some problems associated with a performance standard, the introduction of something new and innovative, or the completion of a specific project. (We will deal more specifically with the differences in Chapter 6.)

Guidelines for Writing Objectives

We have developed sixteen guidelines for writing objectives to aid in their formulation. Please recognize that these are "guidelines" and not "prescriptions." Some of them may not apply or may be relatively unimportant as related to your objectives. You may choose not to consider certain guidelines as you prepare your objectives, which is fine provided that is a conscious decision. Our main purpose here is to make certain you do not overlook the obvious. Also, many of these guidelines were prepared for use in applications that might be broader than in performance appraisal.

Under normal circumstances, a well-formulated objective meets the following criteria:

1. It starts with the word *to,* followed by an accomplishment verb (e.g., "To complete," "To implement," "To reach agreement.")

2. It specifies a single measurable key result to be accomplished.

3. It specifies a target date or a time span for its accomplishment.

4. It specifies maximum cost factors ($ and/or hours). (This needs to be considered for your own planning even if there is no organizational requirement that costs be identified in your objectives.)

5. It is as specific and quantitative (and hence measurable and verifiable) as possible. (The Indicator step is especially useful here.)

6. It specifies only the "what" and "when"; it avoids venturing into the "why" and "how."

7. It relates directly to the accountable manager's roles and missions and to higher level roles, missions, and objectives.

8. It is readily understandable by those who will be contributing to its attainment.

9. It is realistic and attainable, but still represents a significant challenge.

10. It provides maximum payoff on the required investment in time and resources, as compared with other objectives being considered.

11. It is consistent with the resources available or anticipated.

12. It avoids or minimizes dual accountability for achievement when joint effort is required.

13. It is consistent with basic organizational policies and practices.

14. It is willingly agreed to by both supervisor and employee, without undue pressure or coercion.

15. It is recorded in writing, with a copy kept and periodically referred to by both supervisor and employee.

16. It is communicated not only in writing, but also in face-to-face discussions between the accountable manager and those individuals who will be contributing to its attainment.

Key Questions for Evaluating Objectives
Use the following questions for your own evaluation of your objectives or as a guide for your colleagues as they assist in that evaluation.

1. Is the objective statement constructed properly? To (accomplishment verb) (single key result) by (target date or time span) at (cost—$/hours)?

2. Is it measurable and verifiable?

3. Does it relate directly to the accountable manager's roles and missions and to higher level roles, missions, and objectives?

4. Can it be readily understood by those who must implement it?

5. Is the objective a realistic and attainable one that still represents a significant challenge to the accountable manager and his or her organizational unit?

6. Will the result, when achieved, justify the expenditure of time and resources required to achieve it?

7. Is the objective consistent with basic organizational policies and practices?

8. Can the accountability for final results be clearly established?

SUMMARY

This, then, is a "quickie" look at the MOR process, with particular emphasis on the three activities having the greatest influence on appraisal and development: determining key results areas, identifying and specifying indicators, and selecting and setting objectives. These are especially helpful in clarifying the kinds of things to be included in any advance agreement related to performance.

We will be referring to these various steps periodically during the remaining chapters of this book. Our purpose here is to provide a quick refresher for those already familiar with the MOR process and a brief overview for those who are not. For those who want to learn more about the MOR process, we recommend the book, *Management by Objectives and Results for Business and Industry.*

4

Appraisal Models— The Tailored Approach

In Chapter 1, we identified the problem of meeting the "ideal" that many organizations are seeking—a standard approach to performance appraisal with a common appraisal form that is equally applicable throughout. We have yet to see a "checkoff" form that would come anywhere near meeting such an ideal. However, many of the more recent approaches that require the entry of job requirements/expectations and another for achievements do provide the kind of flexibility that will permit the tailoring of the process to the specific job and the specific person being evaluated. For such an approach to work, there must be an identification of the major elements of the job (key results areas, critical elements, or whatever term is acceptable), planned accomplishments within each of these elements, plus objectives related to the growth and development of each individual compatible with both personal and organizational needs. The purpose here is to focus attention on the need to establish mutually agreed-upon *performance* targets related to both job output and personal development.

FACTORS FOR EVALUATION

Using a Management by Objectives and Results (MOR) approach, we will develop here a three-sectioned model (a slight variation on the model in the original edition of this book that comes from a much broader experience base) that can be adapted quite easily to any existing performance appraisal system that permits the kind of flexibility described above. We will develop this model first, then a variation using the MOR Agreement format described in *Management by Objectives and Results for Business and Industry,* and, finally, an alternative for jobs with similar and repetitive responsibilities. We will call the three sections in the first model (1) key results areas, (2) work objectives and assignments, and (3) personal development objectives.

Key Results Areas

The first step in tailoring the approach is to break down the specific job into its major performance elements. In order to keep this approach consistent with MOR, we are using the term *key results areas* here. However, since the "label" is not important but the "process" is, feel free to substitute *performance elements, critical elements, functional requirements, major responsibilities,* or any other terms that represent categories of effort within which results need to be achieved.

As we pointed out in Chapter 3, *key* results areas are just that. They do not cover everything an individual does; such a list would be unmanageable. They identify those areas where *results,* not activities, are significant enough to warrant special attention. See "Guidelines for determining key results areas" on page 28 for assistance in defining these for yourself. Most people will develop a list of five to ten key results areas, but you may wish to limit the number, particularly in the early stages of implementation.

The ideal way to develop a list of key results areas is for the employee and the supervisor to each come up with such a list independently and then compare them, resolving any differences. If this is done in an open exploratory manner, it frequently results in a meaningful dialogue between the two that leads to a more useful and productive list of key results areas than either would have developed on their own. If independent preparation is not a practical alternative, our next recommendation is for the employee to develop his or her own list in draft form, discuss the key results areas with the supervisor and make whatever modifications are appropriate based on that discussion. As a last resort, the supervisor may develop a list of key results areas *for* the employee. This might be appropriate with an employee who is new to the job or one who is marginal or unsatisfactory and may be unable or unwilling to prepare her or his own list.

Once there is agreement, or at least mutual understanding of the key results areas, priorities need to be established for each. This could be done by placing them in rank order, using a number or letter system (e.g., 1 = most important, 2 = important, 3 = desirable, etc.), or following a method several organizations have found especially useful—spreading one hundred points over the list to show the relative importance. For example, a Buyer in the Procurement Office of a large company might identify the following key results areas, each followed by a number representing its relative importance:

Contract Administration and Vendor Surveillance—40

User Requirements Analysis—15

Vendor Identification and Analysis—15

Contract Negotiation—10

Special Projects—20

This prioritization helps put the elements of the job in proper perspective and, once agreement is reached, enables both the employee and the supervisor to focus their efforts accordingly. The numbers and, in some cases, the key results areas themselves may change during the year as both parties recognize and agree that circumstances have changed. The opportunity to reevaluate a performance agreement, based on changing requirements, is essential if the performance appraisal process is to avoid becoming another meaningless paper exercise.

Work Objectives and Assignments

The second section of our appraisal model identifies those specific objectives and assignments for which the employee is to be held accountable during the projected appraisal period. (For clarification purposes here, "objectives" are those work-related activities that have specific measurable end results and which both the supervisor and the employee play a part in formulating and establishing; "assignments" are those predetermined activities for which an employee is made accountable on the supervisor's decision alone or which may be more activity- than results-oriented. There is a place for both in the normal supervisor-employee relationship.)

As was stated earlier, the fact that one individual is being held accountable for a particular objective or assignment does not mean that he or she will be the only one responsible for working on it. It merely means that that employee will be the one accountable to the supervisor for its accomplishment, whether as a result of the employee's effort alone or in cooperation with others. By the same reasoning, that individual is not expected to limit efforts only to those activities for which she or he is held accountable. *There is a reciprocal responsibility for supporting those of other employees as well.* This is critical to an effective team operation and each individual has to recognize his or her obligations. If this is a potential problem with one or more employees, you may wish to include another key results area such as "team effort/support," or have the employee set a personal development objective related to that.

In Chapter 3, we identified a distinction between objectives and performance standards. Performance standards were described as "the achievement and/or maintenance of a level of performance in ongoing efforts such as quality, productivity, cost control, etc." Objectives were referred to as "accomplishments that may or may not be of an ongoing nature.'' We will show how these might be used with this distinction in an alternative model later in this chapter. If you or your organization prefer to use the term *performance standards* to describe what we are calling *objectives,* then by all means do so. The label is not important. What is important is that you identify the specific results to be achieved by the employee.

We also listed sixteen guidelines for writing objectives in Chapter 3. It may prove helpful to review these (see page 33) and use them as you and the employee develop the list of objectives and assignments to be included, recognizing that some of these guidelines may be either not applicable or not important enough to warrant consideration.

Using our illustration of a buyer in a Procurement Office, we might find the following work objectives and assignments as appropriate (note that they logically relate to one or more of the designated key results areas):

1. To administer and ensure vendor compliance with the following existing contracts at an average cost of ten to twenty hours per week:
   a. Arnett Engineering Corporation #82-1466932
   b. Arnett Engineering Corporation #83-0096521
   c. Bracken Supply and Maintenance Co. #83-0099414
   d. Cosmopolitan Services, Inc. #83-0104661
   e. Miscellaneous small contracts as assigned

2. To service the general procurement needs of all field service departments at an average of five hours per week.

3. To determine specifications, let bids, and negotiate contract on the Argenta project by March 1 within budget restrictions with an estimated 120 hours of effort.

4. To survey the field and submit by December 1 a report identifying available area vendors qualifying as small businesses who can provide management training to our specifications at a survey cost not to exceed $100 and forty work-hours.

5. To serve as secretary to the Company's Make-or-Buy Committee at an average cost of ten hours per month.

6. To provide technical training and supervision to one Buyer Intern, as assigned, at an average cost of five to ten hours per week.

Personal Development Objectives

Our appraisal model is completed with a discussion, joint agreement, and commitment on the part of the employee to specific objectives designed to improve over-all capability and value both to the organization and to the employee's own career enhancement. The activities identified here are neither limited to nor excluded from the normal work activities of the group. Normally, these activities will come as a result of joint examination of the employee's career goals and will encompass any or all of the following: correction of performance deficiencies, increased performance capability in present position, and preparation for possible future responsibilities.

Probably the majority of objectives set here will be related to specific activities the employee can perform on the job. In many cases, they will be identical to or in support of objectives and assignments listed earlier. They also may include some of the "Practical Employee Development Activities" identified in Chapter 7 (pages 96–98). In any event, they will be *performance* oriented and compatible with the organization's and department's roles, missions, and objectives and with the employee's career goals. Additional personal development objectives which our buyer might pursue could include:

1. To complete Effective Presentations course by December 31 at a cost not to exceed the registration fee and related expenses and thirty work-hours.

2. To complete Procurement Price/Cost Analysis course by March 31 at a cost not to exceed the registration fee and related expenses and forty work-hours.

3. To develop by November 30 a workable set of guidelines and standards for on-the-job training of Buyer Interns at a cost not to exceed twenty work-hours.

4. To serve on program committee of local chapter of NAPM (National Association of Purchasing Management) at an average cost of four to six hours per month.

VARIATION USING MOR AGREEMENT

In *Management by Objectives and Results for Business and Industry,* we introduced the concept of a one-page MOR Agreement as the document for recording an individual's commitment to her or his supervisor on the primary accomplishments projected. For those organizations who may be using that as a part of their normal MOR implementation efforts, here is a variation on the appraisal model using the MOR Agreement for the Buyer that we used to illustrate the three-sectioned approach. Figure 4.1 shows how that would be developed.

AN ALTERNATIVE MODEL

George Odiorne (see Bibliography) has identified three levels of objectives that might be useful in developing an alternative performance appraisal model,

Fig. 4.1 Buyer's MOR agreement from 10/1 to 9/30.

Key Results Areas Indicators	Objectives
Contract Administration and Vendor Surveillance (40) Assigned contracts	1. To administer and ensure vendor compliance with the following existing contracts at an average cost of ten to twenty hours per week: a. Arnett Engineering Corporation #82-1466932 b. Arnett Engineering Corporation #83-0096521 c. Bracken Supply and Maintenance Co. #83-0099414 d. Cosmopolitan Services, Inc. #83-0104661 e. Miscellaneous small contracts as assigned
User Requirements Analysis (15) Field service needs	2. To service the general procurement needs of all field service departments at an average of five hours per week.
Contract Negotiation (10) Argenta project contract	3. To determine specifications, let bids, and negotiate contract on Argenta project by March 1 within budget restrictions with an estimated 120 hours of effort.
Vendor Identification and Analysis (15) Survey—management training	4. To survey the field and submit by December 1 a report identifying available area vendors qualifying as small businesses who can provide management training to our specifications at a survey cost not to exceed $100 and forty work-hours.
Special Projects (20) Make-or-buy committee	5. To serve as secretary to the company's Make-or-Buy Committee at an average cost of ten hours per month.
Buyer Intern training	6. To provide technical training and supervision to one Buyer Intern, as assigned, at an average cost of five to ten hours per week.
Personal Development Course completions	7. To complete Effective Presentations course by December 31 at a cost not to exceed the registration fee and related expenses and thirty work-hours.
	8. To complete Procurement Price/Cost Analysis course by March 31 at a cost not to exceed the registration fee and related expenses and forty work-hours.
Buyer-Intern training guidelines	9. To develop by November 30 a workable set of guidelines and standards for on-the-job training of Buyer Interns at a cost not to exceed twenty work-hours.
NAPM committee participation	10. To serve on program committee of local chapter of NAPM (National Association of Purchasing Management) at an average cost of four to six hours per month.

PROGRESS REVIEW SCHEDULE 12/1, 2/1, 4/1, 6/1, 8/1

particularly for a job where a significant amount of the work is ongoing and repetitive in nature. The first and most basic level is what he calls *regular or routine objectives.* These represent the normal, ongoing tasks for which there is already established an acceptable level of output. In most organizations, much of this work is already being performed satisfactorily (in some cases *in spite of* rather than *because of* the supervisor's efforts).

Problem-solving objectives, the second level, are focused largely on correcting problems that arise in connection with the regular or routine objectives. For example, if an individual has a regular objective to produce a series of statistical reports with a 98 percent on-time delivery average and the actual on-time delivery average falls substantially below that for an extended period, a problem-solving objective might be established to correct whatever might be causing the delivery delays.

The highest level represents *innovative objectives.* These would be objectives related to expanding capability, moving in new directions, making major modifications to existing efforts, etc. Normally, both the potential payoff and the potential risk are considerably higher with innovative objectives.

In working with several organizations, we have found that the Odiorne model works especially well with employees and organizational units that have both similar and repetitive types of work. By making a slight modification in it, substituting "tasks/responsibilities" and "performance standards" for "regular or routine objectives," we can both simplify and standardize the model for use by several people occupying similar jobs. (The subject of "performance standards" is dealt with in detail in Chapter 6.)

As an example, we will use a Personnel Coordinator for a field unit in a large decentralized company. Assume that there are several other people in comparable positions in other field units, each reporting directly to a Personnel Supervisor at the headquarters location, with a "dotted line" relationship to the field unit manager. The most effective way to establish the initial set of performance standards for this group would be to assemble these Coordinators (or a representative group of them) together with their supervisors plus, if appropriate, one or two representatives of field unit management for a brainstorming session. They would first try to reach agreement on what represents a reasonable list of tasks/responsibilities that would be common to all or most of those affected. Then they would try to reach agreement on what are reasonable performance standards that would represent a satisfactory level of expectation for someone in such a position. (There would have to be enough flexibility built in to allow for some adjustment in these standards because of special circumstances, e.g., location, excessively large or small work force, lack of experience in the position, union activity, etc.) Without any attempt at clarifying or justifying our choices, here is a partial list of ideas that might come out of such a meeting.

Tasks/responsibilities	Performance standards
Personnel actions	$X\%$ of paperwork completed within Y days
Grievance/adverse actions	$X\%$ settled by first or second step
Applicants processed	Avg. X per month processed in Y days or less
EEO compliance	All noncompliance complaints resolved in X days
Personnel studies	Assigned studies completed on schedule
Employee counseling	Avg. X hours per month allocated to counseling avg. Y employees on personnel-related issues
Client relations	Minimum once per month contact with each field unit manager/supervisor
Public relations	Avg. one or more public contacts per month for public relations purposes

Such a list obviously would be expanded to cover other important tasks/responsibilities as well, and there may be other performance standards that are more appropriate than some of those identified here. The key to the effectiveness in this approach lies in the active involvement of those affected (in this case the Personnel Coordinators themselves) in the actual determination of the performance standards. If they have had an opportunity to influence the elements covered, they are far more likely to work toward achieving or exceeding them rather than complaining about how useless or unfair the standards are.

These tasks/responsibilities and performance standards then can be incorporated into the appraisal plan for each person with a comparable job and then supplemented with additional items that may be unique or distinctive for a given individual or location. Then, when it comes to assessing performance, it may turn out that the Personnel Coordinator in one office is meeting or exceeding all performance standards except the ones on personnel actions and personnel studies. *Problem-solving objectives* can be established to correct whatever may be causing these deviations. An individual in another office may be doing fine with both of those, but may be having considerable problems with the standard on grievances, perhaps to the point of having had several cases go to arbitration in recent months. A problem-solving objective there might address doing a more effective job of educating supervisors on grievance procedures.

Innovative objectives in one of these offices would depend to a large degree on the people and the environment within which the individual must work, as well as that person's own interests, ability, and imagination. They could include such things as developing and implementing new methods, installing an employee recognition program, providing training in a particular skill area that may be in short supply, or initiating a plan for attracting a greater number of minority and female applicants.

For this particular model, *personal development objectives* can be included in either the *problem-solving* or *innovative* sections, or could be added as another section.

SUMMARY

For any performance appraisal process to work, it must be tailored both to the individual job and to the individual performing that job. The universal "checkoff" type of appraisal form does not allow that kind of flexibility. In this chapter, we have suggested three models that permit the kind of tailoring necessary to make the performance appraisal process a meaningful dialogue and joint commitment on the part of both the supervisor and the employee. The first is a three-sectioned approach that identifies key results areas (critical elements, major responsibilities, etc.) and the relative importance of each, work objectives and assignments, and personal development objectives. The second is a variation on that using the MOR Agreement format. The third is for jobs that have similar and repetitive factors. Here we identify the tasks/responsibilities and performance standards for those repetitive factors and then encourage the establishment of one or more problem-solving and innovative objectives as well. On the next several pages, we have taken two positions, a Project Planner and a Management Development Specialist, and illustrated how each of the three models might be applied to each of those positions (Figs. 4.2 through 4.7). Obviously, the specific content for each would vary substantially from organization to organization. Our purpose here is to demonstrate the use of the models, not to recommend specific content. As you get ready to establish a plan for a specific *individual* position in your area, select and/or modify the model and the content that will be most useful to you. We will discuss the application of tailored models to *managerial* positions in Chapter 5. We will also have a more in-depth analysis of performance standards and their uses in Chapter 6.

Fig. 4.2 Appraisal and development model—Sample 1a.

Position <u>Project Planner</u>   Incumbent <u>Tom Williams</u>   Supervisor <u>Joe Martin</u>

1. *Key Results Areas*

   Project Performance Surveillance—20
   Statistical Analysis—20
   Budget Projections—10
   Status Reports—20
   Forecast Charts—10
   Special Projects—20

2. *Work Objectives and Assignments*

   a. To maintain continuous surveillance over and provide appropriate communication to management regarding budgetary and schedule performance on each project being handled by the group at an average cost of twenty hours per week. To be included:
      1) Continuous review with notification of significant deviations (likely to lead to budget overruns or schedule slippages) to reach the Supervisor within two working days of their occurrence
      2) Weekly projections of anticipated position on human resources, materials, and schedule
      3) Weekly status reports for inclusion in total department report
      4) Preparation and maintenance of related forecast charts

   b. To analyze requirements and prepare budget estimates for next fiscal year, including detailed estimates for first quarter by end of third quarter at a cost not to exceed sixty work-hours.

   c. To produce tentative cost and schedule estimates within prescribed time limits for all new projects being considered for the group at an average cost of ten work-hours.

   d. To assist each specialist in the group with any statistical analyses required in compliance with assigned projects at an average cost of five hours per week.

3. *Personal Development Objectives*

   a. To develop and implement by (date) a plan for organizing and improving the efficiency of personal work flow at no additional cost.

   b. To complete Effective Communications course by (date) and review with Supervisor the implications for the job within budget plus twenty-four work-hours.

   c. To develop and implement by (date) an approach for improving personal dictating practices at no additional cost.

   d. To develop by (date) a plan, in cooperation with Department Manager's administrative assistant, for consolidation of status reporting system, minimizing bottlenecks and duplication at a cost not to exceed forty work-hours.

PROGRESS REVIEW SCHEDULE <u>First Friday of each month</u>

Fig. 4.3 Project planner's MOR agreement for fiscal year (second half)—Sample 1b.

Key Results Areas Indicators	Objectives

Project Performance Surveillance (20)
   Continuous review
   Deviation notification
	1. To maintain continuous review of budgetary and schedule performance on each project being handled by the group with notification of significant deviations (likely to lead to budget overruns or schedule slippages) to reach the Supervisor within two working days at an average cost of ten hours per week.

Statistical Analysis (20)
   Weekly projections
   Assistance to specialists
	2. To complete weekly projections of anticipated position on human resources, materials, and schedule at an average cost of four hours per week.

	3. To assist each specialist in the group with any statistical analyses required in compliance with assigned projects at an average cost of five hours per week.

Budget Projections (10)
   Group budget estimates
   Project cost and schedule estimates
	4. To analyze requirements and prepare budget estimates for next fiscal year, including detailed estimates for first quarter, by end of third quarter at a cost not to exceed sixty work-hours.

	5. To produce tentative cost and schedule estimates within prescribed time limits for all new projects being considered for the group at an average cost of ten work-hours.

Status Reports (20)
   Weekly completions
   Accuracy of data
	6. To complete weekly status reports by noon on Friday for inclusion in total department report at an average cost of five hours per week.

Forecast Charts (10) Timeliness, accuracy	7. To prepare and maintain all related forecast charts at an average cost of two hours per week.
Special Projects (10)	8. To develop by (date) a plan, in cooperation with Department Manager's administrative assistant, for consolidation of status reporting system at a cost not to exceed forty work-hours.

Personal Development (10)
   Implementation of plans
   Completion of course
	9. To develop and implement by (date) a plan for organizing and improving the efficiency of personal work flow at no additional cost.

	10. To complete Effective Communications course by (date) and review the implications for the job within budget and with an investment of twenty-four work-hours.
	11. To develop and implement by (date) an approach for improving personal dictating practices at no additional cost.

PROGRESS REVIEW SCHEDULE First Friday of each month

Fig. 4.4 Appraisal and development model using performance standards—Sample 1c.

Position <u>Project Planner</u>   Incumbent <u>Tom Williams</u>   Supervisor <u>Joe Martin</u>

Tasks/Responsibilities	*Performance Standards*
Project Performance Surveillance	1. Continuous review; notification of significant deviations (overruns, slippages) to reach Supervisor within two working days.
Statistical Analysis	2. Assistance to specialists as required.
	3. Statistical projections completed weekly.
Budget Projections	4. Next FY budget estimates plus detailed estimates for first quarter completed by end of third quarter.
	5. Project cost and schedule estimates as required.
Status Reports	6. Rough copy by noon on Thursday; final copy (no statistical or arithmetic errors) by noon on Friday.
Forecast Charts	7. Prepared and kept current weekly.
Special Projects	8. Completed as assigned.

Problem-Solving Objectives

Performance Standard #6 not being met.
1. To develop and implement by (date) a plan for organizing and improving the efficiency of personal work flow at no additional cost.
2. To develop and implement by (date) an approach for improving personal dictating practices at no additional cost.

Innovative Objectives

1. To develop by (date) a plan, in cooperation with Department Manager's administrative assistant for consolidation of status reporting system at a cost not to exceed forty work-hours.

Personal Development Objectives

1. To complete Effective Communications course by (date) and review the implications for the job with Supervisor within budget and with an investment of twenty-four work-hours.

PROGRESS REVIEW SCHEDULE <u>First Friday of each month</u>

Fig. 4.5 Appraisal and development model—Sample 2a.

Pos. <u>Mgt. Development Specialist</u> Incumbent <u>Mitchell Blake</u> Supvr. <u>Ann Carr</u>

1. *Key Results Areas*

   Needs Analysis—5
   Program Design and Development—30
   Teaching—30
   Program Administration—25
   Special Projects—10

2. *Work Objectives and Assignments*

   a. To produce a minimum of 7,350 student-hours in management training, within established budget, apportioned as follows:

   | | | | Student-Hours | |
Program	Cycles	Hours	Co. Time	After Hours
(1) Mid-Management Workshop	6	24	1,440	720
(2) Basic Supervisory Training	3	64	3,840	
(3) Leadership Workshop (Engineering)	3	30		1,350

   b. To conduct a needs analysis of at least 20 percent of Mid-Management Workshop graduates by March 31, at a cost not to exceed thirty work-hours, to determine critical additional training requirements for middle managers.

   c. To develop and implement a lesson plan for discussing community action responsibilities in all existing management training programs by February 15 at a cost not to exceed twenty work-hours.

   d. To develop by April 15, at a cost not to exceed thirty work-hours, and maintain thereafter a systematic approach to reviewing, summarizing, and recording results of student objectives.

   e. To develop and implement by May 31 a working plan for distribution of management education literature to management training graduates—implementation cost not to exceed ten work-hours and department publication budget.

   f. To serve as department representative on the Management Club's management development committee at a cost not to exceed four work-hours per month.

3. *Personal Development Objectives*

   a. To complete programmed instruction course in Essentials of Accounting by June 30 at cost of enrollment fee with no work-hour allocation.

   b. To prepare and present to a meeting of the American Society for Training and Development a demonstration workshop on "On-the-Job Measurement of Supervisory Training" by June 30 at a cost not to exceed twenty work-hours.

   c. To develop an integrated staff/loading plan for the next quarter in the management training group by March 15 at a cost not to exceed ten work-hours.

PROGRESS REVIEW SCHEDULE <u>First Monday of each month</u>

Fig. 4.6 Management development specialist's MOR agreement for fiscal year (first half)—Sample 2b.

Key Results Areas Indicators	Objectives
Needs Analysis (5) Survey of Mid-Management graduates completed	1. To conduct a needs analysis of at least 20 percent of Mid-Management Workshop graduates by March 31, at a cost not to exceed thirty work-hours, to determine critical additional training requirements for middle managers.
Program Design and Development (30) Lesson plan implemented	2. To develop and implement a lesson plan for discussing community action responsibilities in all existing management training programs by February 15 at a cost not to exceed twenty work-hours.
Teaching (30) Student-hours produced	3. To produce a minimum of 7,350 student-hours in management training, within established budget, apportioned as follows:

Program	Cycles	Hours	Student-Hours Co. Time	After Hours
(1) Mid-Management Workshop	6	24	1,440	720
(2) Basic Supervisory Training	3	64	3,840	
(3) Leadership Workshop (Engineering)	3	30		1,350

Program Administration (25) Student objectives followup Literature plan implemented	4. To develop by April 15, at a cost not to exceed thirty work-hours, and maintain thereafter a systematic approach to reviewing, summarizing, and recording results of student objectives.
	5. To develop and implement by May 31 a working plan for distribution of management education literature to management training graduates —implementation cost not to exceed ten workhours and department publication budget.
Special Projects (10) Management Club service	6. To serve as department representative on the Management Club's management development committee at a cost not to exceed four workhours per month.
Personal Development Course completed ASTD presentation Staff/loading plan developed	7. To complete programmed instruction course in Essentials of Accounting by June 30 at cost of enrollment fee with no work-hours.
	8. To prepare and present to a meeting of the American Society for Training and Development a demonstration workshop on "On-the-Job Measurement of Supervisory Training" by June 30 at a cost not to exceed twenty work-hours.
	9. To develop an integrated staff/loading plan for the next quarter in the management training group by March 15 at a cost not to exceed ten work-hours.

PROGRESS REVIEW SCHEDULE First Monday of each month

Fig. 4.7 Appraisal and development model using performance standards—Sample 2c.

Pos. <u>Mgt. Development Specialist</u>   Incumbent <u>Mitchell Blake</u>   Supvr. <u>Ann Carr</u>

Tasks/Responsibilities   *Performance Standards*

Needs Analysis   1. Graduates surveyed for additional needs.

Program Design and   2. Assigned lesson plans developed and implemented.
Development

Teaching   3. Specified class sessions taught.

                               4. Specified student-hours produced:

| | | | Student-Hours | |
Program	Cycles	Hours	Co. Time	After Hours
(1) Mid-Management Workshop	6	24	1,440	720
(2) Basic Supervisory Training	3	64	3,840	
(3) Leadership Workshop (Engineering)	3	30		1,350

Program   5. Minimum enrollments met.
Administration
                     6. Records completed within one week.

                     7. Systematic on-the-job follow-up of student perfor-
                        mance.

Special Projects   8. Assigned projects completed on schedule.

Problem-Solving Objectives

Performance Standard #1 not being met.
1. To conduct a needs analysis of at least 20 percent of Mid-Management Workshop graduates by March 31, at a cost not to exceed thirty work-hours, to determine critical additional training requirements for middle managers.

Performance Standard #7 not being met.
2. To develop by April 15, at a cost not to exceed thirty work-hours, and maintain
   thereafter a systematic approach to reviewing, summarizing, and recording results of student objectives.

Innovative Objectives

1. To develop and implement by May 31 a working plan for distribution of
   management education literature to management training graduates—implementation cost not to exceed ten work-hours and department publication budget.
2. To prepare and present to a meeting of the American Society for Training and
   Development a demonstration workshop on "On-the-Job Measurement of Supervisory Training" by June 30 at a cost not to exceed twenty work-hours.

Personal Development Objectives

1. To complete programmed instruction course in Essentials of Accounting by June
   30 at cost of enrollment fee with no work-hours.
2. To develop an integrated staff/loading plan for the next quarter in the management training group by March 15 at a cost not to exceed ten work-hours.

PROGRESS REVIEW SCHEDULE <u>First Monday of each month</u>

5

Manager/Supervisor Appraisal and Development

We shall be examining manager/supervisor appraisal and development from the perspective of the individual member of management (at whatever level) who is held accountable for the output of one or more work units as well as for the performance of employees within those units. Performance appraisal is not, and should not be seen as, "another Personnel program." While Personnel (or some other designated staff organization) may have the responsibility for administering and coordinating it, any performance appraisal effort must be perceived as a supervisory management responsibility. In the final analysis, it is the individual manager/supervisor who is held accountable for the appraisal and development of the people in her or his organization, including lower level members of management.

SIMILARITIES TO EMPLOYEE APPRAISAL AND DEVELOPMENT

In many ways, there are no differences, conceptually or practically, between the appraisal and development of managers and the appraisal and development of other employees. All of the principles and techniques covered throughout this book are equally applicable to individual members of management who, of course, are also *employees*. As such, they are entitled to the same consideration from top management, their supervisors, and appropriate staff organizations. In addition, they have the same responsibilities for their own development with the added factor of setting a good example for those who report to them. Although these observations are self-evident, all too often we see evidence that middle managers and above, while expressing a concern for employee development within their organizations, overlook their own obligations for the individual members of *management* who report directly to them.

DIFFERENCES FROM EMPLOYEE APPRAISAL AND DEVELOPMENT

While, in many ways, there may be no differences between the appraisal and development of managers and that of other employees, the nature of the factors to be considered and the complexity of the process itself require that the application to an individual member of management be treated separately. Probably the most significant difference is that the appraisal and development of a manager/supervisor is related more to his or her impact on the output of others than on personal output. Also, many of the factors are considerably less tangible than those related to most individual employees. Therefore, perhaps even more than with the individual employee, the manager needs to be reviewed in terms of results produced and how well she or he performs against mutually accepted objectives. This makes the objective-setting part of the appraisal and development process an even more critical step.

As we see it, there are four general areas in which the appraisal and development process has meaning for the individual manager. Not necessarily in order of importance, these are: unit output, self output, performance in the functions of management, and performance and development of that individual's employees.

Unit Output

In one sense, this is really the measure of managerial effectiveness. The actual output in terms of products and services of the work unit(s) for which that manager is accountable is the most obvious payoff. Presumably, it represents the results of managerial efforts to marshall the various available resources toward fulfillment of the roles, missions, and objectives of the organization. We would be among the last to suggest that this was the sole measure of managerial value, or that there might not be several other factors that could have either a positive or negative effect on output. However, we are kidding ourselves if we do not consider this a major indicator of how well a manager is performing and where improvement efforts should be directed. Unless the manager is concerned with the specific contribution being made by the unit toward the economic and service motives of the organization, and unless this is one of the prime areas of appraisal and development discussion with her or his supervisor, it is difficult, if not impossible, to justify that person's role as a member of management.

Self Output

Regardless of an individual's level in the managerial hierarchy or the number of people supervised, every manager has certain elements of output for which he or she is personally accountable. These outputs are, at best, only indirectly related to that person's role as a member of management. They could be technical in nature, they could involve such things as client or vendor relations, or they could represent certain specific skills which that individual is especially well qualified to use.

In addition to the efforts that are directly or indirectly related to unit output, every member of management also performs certain *staff* functions as well. Thus, each manager might be called on to represent the organization at certain functions, to provide advice and counsel to higher level management on key issues and to perform specific supportive actions within that relationship, to serve as a member of an advisory group which would include participation in staff meetings with other managers, and to perform certain specific assignments that are for the good of the total organization but are not directly related to that manager's primary responsibilities. For some managers this may take up a significant proportion of their time and effort; for others it may not. It is a natural and necessary part of every manager's job, however, and needs to be considered and placed in perspective as it relates to that manager's appraisal and development.

The nature and extent of a manager's self-output will vary widely, of course, but whatever they may be, the manager must make a cost-benefit analysis of the impact of self-output efforts on managerial efforts. This relationship needs to be clearly understood in advance by the manager and his or her supervisor. Otherwise, there may be the temptation on the part of the manager to let self-output efforts become disproportionate to managerial efforts.

The problem with manager/supervisor appraisal in many, if not most, organizations is that virtually all attention is focused on *unit output* and *self-output* as the assessment of that manager's contributions. While we do not mean to downplay their importance, they represent only a portion of the potential impact from the manager's efforts. Furthermore, the impact from contributions made in those two areas tends to be short term in nature. We feel it is equally important that a manager's performance appraisal should give substantial attention to how well she or he performs in the functions of management and in relation to the performance and development of the people in his or her work unit.

Performance in the Functions of Management

While measurement of unit output is certainly one way of measuring a manager's effectiveness in performing in the functions of management, it needs to be examined more specifically from the perspective of appraisal and development. The manager's demonstration of ability to perform more effectively and to gain higher level perspectives within these functions will, perhaps more than anything else, indicate that person's degree of readiness for positions of greater responsibility.

In *Management by Objectives and Results for Business and Industry* we identified the five functions and nineteen distinct activities that go into management work. The following is a review of them:

Function 1. Planning.   Determining what work must be done.

1. *Defining roles and missions.*   Determining the nature and scope of the work to be performed.

2. *Determining key results areas.*   Determining where to invest time, energy, talent, and other resources.

3. *Identifying and specifying indicators of effectiveness.*   Determining measurable factors on which objectives may be set.

4. *Selecting and setting objectives.*   Determining results to be achieved.

5. *Preparing action plans.*   Determining how to achieve specific objectives.
   a. *Programming.*   Establishing a sequence of actions to follow in reaching objectives.
   b. *Scheduling.*   Establishing time requirements for objectives and action steps.
   c. *Budgeting.*   Determining and assigning the resources required to reach objectives.
   d. *Fixing accountability.*   Determining who will see to the accomplishment of objectives and action steps.
   e. *Reviewing and reconciling.*   Testing and revising a tentative plan, as needed, prior to commitment to action.

6. *Policy making.*   Establishing rules, regulations, or predetermined decisions.

7. *Establishing procedures.*   Determining consistent and systematic methods of handling work.

Function II. Organizing.   Classifying and dividing the work into manageable units.

1. *Structuring.*   Grouping the work for effective and efficient production.

2. *Integrating.*   Establishing conditions for effective teamwork among organizational units.

Function III. Staffing.   Determining the requirements for and ensuring the availability of personnel to perform the work.

1. *Determining personnel needs.*   Analyzing the work for personnel capabilities required.

2. *Selecting personnel.*   Identifying and appointing people to organizational positions.

3. *Developing personnel.*   Providing opportunities for people to increase their capabilities in line with organizational needs.

Function IV. Directing (leading).   Bringing about the human activity required to accomplish objectives.

1. *Assigning.*   Charging individual employees with job responsibilities or specific tasks to be performed.

2. *Motivating.*   Influencing people to perform in a desired manner.

3. *Communicating.*   Achieving effective flow of ideas and information in all desired directions.

4. *Coordinating.*   Achieving harmony of group effort toward the accomplishment of individual and group objectives.

Function V. Controlling.   Ensuring the effective accomplishment of objectives.

1. *Establishing standards.*   Devising a gauge of successful performance in achieving objectives.

2. *Measuring performance.*   Assessing actual versus planned performance.

3. *Taking corrective action.*   Bringing about performance improvement toward objectives.[1]

Each of the functions and activities identified here is performed by every manager/supervisor at every level. The differences are ones of magnitude and frequency. Figure 5.1[2] shows the variation in the percentage of effort devoted to each of the five functions at three levels of management.

As is readily apparent from the illustration, the biggest variation in proportionate effort is in the directing function. The closer the manager is to the unit's direct output, the larger is the proportion of effort likely to be devoted to the directing function. Conversely, the further away from this output, the less time and effort should be devoted to directing and more attention given to the other functions. Obviously, the actual mix of the various functions will not be as smooth as in Fig. 5.1 and will be influenced by other factors as well. Nevertheless, the marked change in the mix as a manager proceeds up the management ladder is inescapable. Therefore, a highly successful first-line supervisor will not necessarily make a good middle manager; nor, on the other hand, will a middle manager who possesses the necessary skills to perform effectively at that level be a guaranteed success as a first-line supervisor. They are different jobs.

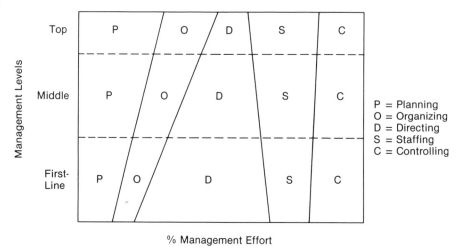

Fig. 5.1 Proportion of management effort devoted to planning, organizing, directing, staffing, and controlling.

The manner in which the manager's performance in these functions and activities is to be appraised and development objectives are to be set must be tailored to the situation, of course. However, it appears obvious that specific attention must be given to this area in the appraisal and development of any manager/supervisor.

Performance and Development of Employees

While this particular factor has been identified to some extent, it needs to be dealt with separately because of its particular importance in assessing the role of a manager. Since a manager is only as effective as the people in his or her work unit, it stands to reason that the ability to achieve meaningful performance from—and to assist in the development of—those employees should be a significant consideration in that manager's appraisal and in the determination of improvement needs. Yet all too often, little if any attention is given to a manager's performance in this area until a crisis arises in which the manager's shortcomings become obvious (no qualified replacements for critical positions, good employees leaving, marginal employees remaining marginal, etc.). At this time, of course, it is too late to do anything other than criticize the manager for those failures. If performance in this vital area were treated as an integral part of overall appraisal and development considerations, there might be a more concentrated effort on the part of a much larger number of managers to do a more professional job related to the performance and development of their employees.

APPLYING THE MODELS TO MANAGERIAL POSITIONS

Using the three models (three-sectioned, MOR Agreement, performance standards) described in Chapter 4, we will illustrate the application with three fairly typical positions in relatively large organizations: a Supervisor of Technical Services (Headquarters unit), an Area Sales Manager, and a Human Resource Development Manager. We will describe each situation briefly and then apply all three models to each to demonstrate the comparative use. In order to provide as broad a perspective as possible, we have largely avoided using specific technical illustrations requiring extensive explanation. Obviously, similar positions in your organization would be much more specific and would be tailored to your exact requirements. Concentrate primarily on the use of each of the models and which one, or what modification, would be most useful to you, rather than the specific content. Also, please note that there is a designated "Progress Review Schedule" on each model. We believe this is just as essential to the agreement as the content itself.

Position 1: Supervisor of Technical Services

Marilyn McGregor is Supervisor of a Technical Services group in a moderate-sized company. She is a "working supervisor" with about half of her present duties technical in nature and half devoted to supervising the work of the four technicians and one clerical person who report to her. Her position was created when the group was expanded about a year ago. She reports to Ardis Allen, Manager of Technical Operations. Marilyn's work as a technician has been exemplary over the five years she has been with the company and she was the logical choice when the supervisory position was created. The others in her group, including a new technician who was hired last month, like her and respect her technical ability. Because her technical skills are so good, she is reluctant to give up some of the work she has been involved in and, as a result, she is overworked while some of her people are underutilized. She and her supervisor have discussed this and reached a mutual agreement on her performance appraisal and development plan for the coming year. Figures 5.2, 5.3, and 5.4 show samples of how this plan would look using each of the three models described in Chapter 4.

Position 2: Area Sales Manager

Roger Belton is Area Sales Manager accountable for the operation of ten local offices of a technical field sales department for a large company. He reports to Greg Miller, Regional Manager, who reports to Lynn Caldwell, Director of Field Sales at Headquarters. Roger has been in that position for several years and, in addition to the ten local office supervisors reporting to him, he has two technical program coordinators, an administrative assistant, and a clerk-typist in his office. Roger has become "comfortable" in his job and, in the opinion of his supervisor, spends too much time in the office and not enough in assist-

Fig. 5.2 Appraisal and development model—Sample 1a.

Pos. <u>Technical Services Supvr.</u>   Incumbent <u>Marilyn McGregor</u>   Supvr. <u>Ardis Allen</u>

1. *Key Results Areas*

   Unit Output—25
   Personal Output—25
   User Relations—5
   Productivity—10
   Quality Control—5
   Performance in Functions of Management—10
   Performance and Development of Employees—10
   Self-Development—10

2. *Work Objectives and Assignments*

   a. To meet all production output requirements for the group as specified in the department business plan within existing budget.

   b. To maintain personal control over all Headquarters projects, delegating responsibility for all others to staff, at a personal investment of fifteen to twenty work-hours per week.

   c. To reach agreement, by end of first quarter, with all user contact people outside of Headquarters, on transfer of project responsibility to other group staff members, at an investment of twenty hours of my time.

   d. To increase average output per individual group member (excluding me) by a minimum of 10 percent by end of first quarter, increasing to 20 percent by end of second quarter, at no increase in cost.

   e. To maintain a production error level of no more than 3 percent at no increase in cost.

   f. To have at least two members of the group qualified to perform each major assignment (including ones currently handled by me) by end of second quarter within current training budget and at an on-the-job training cost not to exceed four hours per week of my time and two hours per week of each other technician.

3. *Personal Development Objectives*

   a. To reduce my direct involvement in technical work from approximately 60 percent of my time to no more than 30 percent (with corresponding increase in time allocated to management responsibilities) by end of third quarter at no increase in cost.

   b. To complete Effective Leadership training and apply at least three specific concepts to the job by end of first quarter within current training budget and at an investment of twenty-four work-hours.

PROGRESS REVIEW SCHEDULE <u>Third Friday of each month</u>

Fig. 5.3 Technical services supervisor's MOR agreement for fiscal year—Sample 1b.

Key Results Areas Indicators	Objectives
Unit Output (25) Department business plan	1. To meet all production output requirements for the group as specified in the department business plan within existing budget.
Personal Output (25) Projects controlled	2. To maintain personal control over all Headquarters projects, delegating responsibility for all others to staff, at a personal investment of fifteen to twenty work-hours per week.
User Relations (5) Agreement on transfer of responsibility	3. To reach agreement, by end of first quarter, with all user contact people outside of Headquarters, on transfer of project responsibility to other group staff members, at an investment of twenty hours of my time.
Productivity (10) Output per individual	4. To increase average output per individual group member (excluding me) by a minimum of 10 percent by end of first quarter, increasing to 20 percent by end of second quarter, at no increase in cost.
Quality Control (5) Production error level	5. To maintain a production error level of no more than 3 percent at no increase in cost.
Performance in Functions of Management (10)	(See objectives #1, 2, 4, 5, 6, 7)
Performance & Development of Employees (10) # qualified to perform major assignments	6. To have at least two members of the group qualified to perform each major assignment (including ones currently handled by me) by end of second quarter within current training budget and at an on-the-job training cost not to exceed four hours per week of my time and two hours per week of each other technician.

Self-Development (10)
  % reduction technical work
  Training completed
	7. To reduce my direct involvement in technical work from approximately 60 percent of my time to no more than 30 percent (with corresponding increase in time allocated to management responsibilities) by end of third quarter at no increase in cost.

	8. To complete Effective Leadership training and apply at least three specific concepts to the job by end of first quarter within current training budget and at an investment of twenty-four work-hours.

PROGRESS REVIEW SCHEDULE Third Friday of each month

Fig. 5.4 Appraisal and development model using performance standards—Sample 1c.

Pos. <u>Technical Services Supvr.</u> Incumbent <u>Marilyn McGregor</u> Supvr. <u>Ardis Allen</u>

Tasks/Responsibilities	*Performance Standards*
Department Business Plan	1. Production output requirements met as specified.
Personal Technical Services	2. Direct personal control over HQ projects, all others delegated to staff.
User Relations	3. Non-HQ project responsibility transferred to other staff—agreement reached with user contact people.
Productivity	4. Average output per individual increased 20 percent.
Quality Control	5. Production error level no more than 3 percent.
Performance in Functions of Management	6. Reflected in meeting of performance standards.
Performance & Development of Employees	7. Two persons qualified for each major assignment.

Problem-Solving Objectives

Performance standards #2, 3, 4, 7 not being met.

1. To delegate responsibility for all non-HQ projects to other staff members by end of first quarter.
2. To reach agreement, by end of first quarter, with all user contact people outside of Headquarters, on transfer of project responsibility to other group staff members, at an investment of twenty hours of my time.
3. To increase average output per individual group member (excluding me) by a minimum of 10 percent by end of first quarter, increasing to 20 percent by end of second quarter (requires delegation and training).
4. To have at least two members of the group qualified to perform each major assignment (including ones currently handled by me) by end of second quarter within current training budget and at an on-the-job training cost not to exceed four hours per week of my time and two hours per week of each other technician.

Innovative Objectives

Since several of above objectives require innovative approaches at this time, no additional innovative objectives are projected in this agreement.

Personal Development Objectives

1. To reduce my direct involvement in technical work from approximately 60 percent of my time to no more than 30 percent (with corresponding increase in time allocated to management responsibilities) by end of third quarter at no increase in cost.
2. To complete Effective Leadership training and apply at least three specific concepts to the job by end of first quarter within current training budget and at an investment of twenty-four work-hours.

PROGRESS REVIEW SCHEDULE <u>Third Friday of each month</u>

ing the local office supervisors. Also, there is a big Headquarters push on to reduce selling expense while also improving customer relations. (There are several major customers in the area with whom a periodic management contact is desirable.) Roger and his supervisor have reached a compromise agreement on his performance appraisal and development plan as reflected in Figs. 5.5, 5.6, and 5.7.

Position 3: Human Resource Development Manager

Paul Carter is Manager of Human Resource Development in a large company. He has been in the position for five years, having moved up from Supervisor of Management Training. He has four supervisors reporting to him covering management training, technical and skills training, professional development, and educational programs and services. His performance has been evaluated as well above average by the Vice President of Human Resources to whom he reports. Both Paul and his supervisor agree that there is a need for improving both unit cost and productivity in the HRD department and have agreed on the use of student-hours as a reasonably accurate way of tracking these improvements. They also agree that Paul needs to be more visible with using departments and that those supervisors reporting to Paul need to broaden their understanding of the total HRD function. His performance appraisal and development plan addresses these areas of concern, as shown in Figs. 5.8, 5.9, and 5.10.

USE OF OBJECTIVES AND RESULTS IN MANAGERIAL CAREER PLANNING

Managerial career planning, while directly related to manager development, is really no different from any other planning effort. It requires identification of a career goal which, in effect, becomes a long-range objective. The action plan then becomes the critical activity as it determines the path to be followed to reach the career goal. In this process, of course, each intermediate step along the way can be established as an objective itself and the MOR process is applied. Therefore, the use of objectives and results becomes an integral part of career planning.

As we examine managerial career planning, we need to take a look at it from two perspectives—that of the organization and that of the individual manager. Obviously, the greater the compatibility between these two perspectives, the greater likelihood there is that the plan will succeed.

From the organization's perspective, managerial career planning must be related to long-range needs. Consequently, while planned appraisal and development are a consideration with *every* member of management, managerial career planning, from the organization's perspective, must be exercised on a highly *selective* basis. This leads inevitably to the potential problems in what has come to be called the "crown prince" approach. Although there are many variations in application, depending on top management's point of view, there

Fig. 5.5 Appraisal and development model—Sample 2a.

Position <u>Area Sales Manager</u>   Incumbent <u>Roger Belton</u>   Supervisor <u>Greg Miller</u>

1. *Key Results Areas*

    Financial/Operating Results—20
    Local Office Assistance—15
    Customer Relations—10
    Cost Control—10
    Unit Administration—15
    Performance in Functions of Management—10
    Anticipation/Innovation—5
    Performance and Development of Employees—10
    Self-Development—5

2. *Work Objectives and Assignments*

    a. To produce the financial and operating results as specified in area plan within assigned budget.

    b. To meet with each local office supervisor at least once each month, each meeting to have specific preestablished objectives, at a cost not to exceed travel budget and five work-days per month.

    c. To maintain direct unsolicited contact with not less than ten major customers each month at a monthly cost not to exceed fifteen hours of my time, within approved entertainment budget.

    d. To reduce selling expense to a maximum of 9 percent of gross sales, effective March 1, at an implementation cost not to exceed $500 and one hundred work-hours.

    e. To reduce the amount of my time spent on office administration from a monthly average of eighty hours to no more than thirty hours by end of first quarter with no increase in staff.

    f. To have at least one new service or promotional idea approved and implemented each quarter, with no increase in budget.

    g. To have a mutually agreed on and implemented development plan with at least five of the local office supervisors reporting to me by end of first quarter within existing training budget and at a monthly investment not to exceed thirty hours of my time.

3. *Personal Development Objectives*

    a. To complete self-study program on time management and apply at least two new ideas to my job by end of first quarter within existing training budget and a work-hour investment not to exceed ten hours.

PROGRESS REVIEW SCHEDULE <u>First Friday, even-numbered months</u>

Fig. 5.6 Area sales manager's MOR agreement from 1/1 to 12/31—Sample 2b.

Key Results Areas *Indicators*	*Objectives*
Financial/Operating Results (20) Area plan	1. To produce the financial and operating results as specified in area plan within assigned budget.
Local Office Assistance (15) Meetings with objectives	2. To meet with each local office supervisor at least once each month, each meeting to have specific preestablished objectives, at a cost not to exceed travel budget and five work-days per month.
Customer Relations (10) # customer contacts	3. To maintain direct unsolicited contact with not less than ten major customers each month at a monthly cost not to exceed fifteen hours of my time, within approved entertainment budget.
Cost Control (10) selling expense as % of sales	4. To reduce selling expense to a maximum of 9 percent of gross sales, effective March 1, at an implementation cost not to exceed $500 and one hundred work-hours.
Unit Administration (15) Amount of time spent	5. To reduce the amount of my time spent on office administration from a monthly average of eighty hours to no more than thirty hours by end of first quarter with no increase in staff.
Performance in Functions of Management (10)	(See objectives #1, 2, 5, 7)
Anticipation/Innovation (5) # new ideas implemented	6. To have at least one new service or promotional idea approved and implemented each quarter, with no increase in budget.
Performance & Development of Employees (10) # local office supervisors with development plan	7. To have mutually agreed on and implemented development plan with at least five of the local office supervisors reporting to me by end of first quarter within existing training budget and at a monthly investment not to exceed thirty hours of my time.
Self-Development (5) Self-study program completed	8. To complete self-study program on time management and apply at least two new ideas to my job by end of first quarter within existing training budget and a work-hour investment not to exceed ten hours.

PROGRESS REVIEW SCHEDULE First Friday, even-numbered months

Fig. 5.7 Appraisal and development model using performance standards—Sample 2c.

Position <u>Area Sales Manager</u>   Incumbent <u>Roger Belton</u>   Supervisor <u>Greg Miller</u>

Tasks/Responsibilities	*Performance Standards*
Area Plan	1. Financial and Operating results produced as specified.
Local Office Assistance	2. Individual monthly meetings with objectives.
Customer Relations	3. Contact with 10 major customers per month.
Cost control	4. Selling expense at maximum 9% of gross sales.
Unit Administration	5. Current results maintained with maximum of thirty hours per month of manager's time.
Performance in Functions of Management	6. Reflected in meeting of performance standards.
Performance & Development of Employees	7. Development plans with each local office supervisor.

Problem-Solving Objectives

Performance standards #2, 3, 4, 5, 7 not being met.

1. To meet with each local office supervisor at least once each month beginning immediately, each meeting to have specific preestablished objectives, at a cost not to exceed travel budget and five work-days per month.

2. To maintain direct unsolicited contact with not less than ten major customers each month at a monthly cost not to exceed fifteen hours of my time, within approved entertainment budget.

3. To reduce selling expense to a maximum of 9 percent of gross sales, effective March 1, at an implementation cost not to exceed $500 and one hundred work-hours.

4. To reduce the amount of my time spent on office administration from a monthly average of eighty hours to no more than thirty hours by end of first quarter with no increase in staff. (Requires analysis of current effort for efficiency improvement plus training of and delegation to other office staff.)

5. To have a mutually agreed on and implemented development plan with at least five of the local office supervisors reporting to me by end of first quarter within existing training budget and at a monthly investment not to exceed thirty hours of my time.

Innovative Objectives

1. To have at least one new service or promotional idea approved and implemented each quarter, with no increase in budget.

Personal Development Objectives

1. To complete self-study program on time management and apply at least two new ideas to my job by end of first quarter within existing training budget and a work-hour investment not to exceed ten hours.

PROGRESS REVIEW SCHEDULE <u>First Friday, even-numbered months</u>

Fig. 5.8 Appraisal and development model—Sample 3a.

Pos. <u>Mgr, Human Resource Dev.</u>   Incumbent <u>Paul Carter</u>   Supvr. <u>Gale Wilson</u>

1. *Key Results Areas*

   Operating Results—30
   Cost Control—10
   Productivity—10
   Customer Contact—10
   Performance in Functions of Management—15
   Performance and Development of Employees—10
   Anticipation/Innovation—10
   Self-Development—5

2. *Work Objectives and Assignments*

   a. To produce a minimum of 198,000 student-hours of training while meeting the remainder of the objectives stated in the department operating plan within prescribed budget.

   b. To produce training at a unit cost not to exceed $2.40 per student-hour.

   c. To achieve an approved cost reduction goal of $100,000.

   d. To achieve an average productivity rate of not less than 5,000 student-hours per department employee for the six-month period.

   e. To develop by March 1 and maintain thereafter a regular systematic plan of contact with all using departments for needs analysis and program priority determination purposes at an average cost of ten hours per month of my time.

   f. To maintain, and update quarterly, career development profiles on all members of management at manager level and above and to provide related advice and service as needed at an average cost of ten hours per month of my time and ten hours per month of clerical time.

   g. To implement a short-term exchange of principal duties among department supervisors for development purposes—to involve at least two supervisors each quarter at an average cost of five hours per month of my time.

   h. To establish a jointly sponsored (company and local university) middle management certificate program to start in fall semester within established budget and at an implementation cost not to exceed 200 staff hours (mine and others).

   i. To develop by April 30 a "straw man" five-year plan for establishing an integrated approach to Organization Development within the company at a planning cost not to exceed one hundred staff hours (mine and others).

3. *Personal Development Objectives*

   a. To attend an Organization Development administrators' seminar and prepare a written summary plus an explanatory briefing for related department personnel by March 1 at a cost not to exceed enrollment fees and thirty hours of my time.

   b. To serve as advisor to a company-sponsored Junior Achievement firm at an average monthly cost of twenty hours of my time.

PROGRESS REVIEW SCHEDULE <u>Last working day of each month</u>

Fig. 5.9 HRD manager's MOR agreement from 1/1 to 6/30—Sample 3b.

Key Results Areas Indicators	Objectives

Operating Results (30)
  # student-hours
  Operating plan
	1. To produce a minimum of 198,000 student-hours of training while meeting the remainder of objectives stated in the department operating plan within prescribed budget.

Cost Control (10)
  Unit cost per
  student-hour
  Cost reduction goal
	2. To produce training at a unit cost not to exceed $2.40 per student-hour.
	
	3. To achieve an approved cost reduction goal of $100,000.

Productivity (10)
  Student-hours per
  employee
	4. To achieve an average productivity rate of not less than 5,000 student-hours per department employee for the six-month period.

Customer Contact (10)
  Contact plan
  Career development
  profiles
	5. To develop by March 1 and maintain thereafter a regular systematic plan of contact with all using departments for needs analysis and program priority determination purposes at an average cost of ten hours per month of my time.
	
	6. To maintain, and update quarterly, career development profiles on all members of management at manager level and above and to provide related advice and service as needed at an average monthly cost of ten hours my time and ten clerical hours.

Performance in Mgmt. Functions (15)	(See objectives #1, 2, 3, 4, 7, 9)
Performance and Development of Employees (10) Exchange of duties	7. To implement a short-term exchange of principal duties among department supervisors for development purposes—to involve at least two supervisors each quarter at an average cost of five hours per month of my time.

Anticipation/
Innovation (10)
  Certificate program
  OD plan
	8. To establish a jointly sponsored (company and local university) middle management certificate program to start in fall semester within established budget and at an implementation cost not to exceed 200 staff hours (mine and others).
	
	9. To develop by April 30 a "straw man" five-year plan for establishing an integrated approach to Organization Development within the company at a planning cost not to exceed one hundred staff hours (mine and others).

Self-Development (5)
  Seminar and
  summary
  J.A. advisor service
	10. To attend an Organization Development administrator's seminar and prepare a written summary plus an explanatory briefing for related department personnel by March 1 at a cost not to exceed enrollment fees and thirty hours of my time.
	
	11. To serve as advisor to a company-sponsored Junior Achievement firm at an average monthly cost of twenty hours of my time.

PROGRESS REVIEW SCHEDULE Last working day of each month

Fig. 5.10 Appraisal and development model using performance standards—Sample 3c.

Pos. <u>Mgr, Human Resource Dev.</u>   Incumbent <u>Paul Carter</u>   Supvr. <u>Gale Wilson</u>

Tasks/Responsibilities	*Performance Standards*
Department Operating Plan	1. 198,000 student-hours produced.
	2. Operating plan objectives met.
Cost Control	3. Unit cost—$2.40 per student-hour.
	4. Cost reduction goal of $100,000.
Productivity	5. 5,000 student-hours per dept. employee.
Customer Contact	6. Regular contact with using departments.
	7. Career development profiles maintained.
Performance & Development of Employees	8. Supervisors capable of backing each other up.

Problem-Solving Objectives

Performance standards #3, 5, 6 and 8 not being met.

1. To reduce unit cost of training from $2.75 to $2.40 per student-hour.

2. To increase average productivity rate from 4,450 student-hours per department employee to 5,000 for the six-month period.

3. To develop by March 1 and maintain thereafter a regular systematic plan of contact with all using departments for needs analysis and program priority determination purposes at an average cost of ten hours per month of my time.

4. To implement a short-term exchange of principal duties among department supervisors for development purposes—to involve at least two supervisors each quarter at an average cost of five hours per month of my time.

Innovative Objectives

1. To establish a jointly sponsored (company and local university) middle management certificate program to start in fall semester within established budget and at an implementation cost not to exceed 200 staff hours (mine and others).

2. To develop by April 30 a "straw man" five-year plan for establishing an integrated approach to Organization Development within the company at a planning cost not to exceed one hundred staff hours (mine and others).

Personal Development Objectives

1. To attend an Organization Development administrator's seminar and prepare a written summary plus an explanatory briefing for related department personnel by March 1 at a cost not to exceed enrollment fees and thirty hours of my time.

2. To serve as advisor to a company-sponsored Junior Achievement firm at an average monthly cost of twenty hours of my time.

PROGRESS REVIEW SCHEDULE <u>Last working day of each month</u>

---

are ample indications that many organizations have identified "fast track" performers well before their formal selection for a specialized development program. While philosophically we might espouse the theory that every employee should receive equal opportunity for such development, simple economics make that impractical. Very few, if any, organizations have the time, the training resources, or the available openings to develop everyone. Furthermore, not everyone is anxious to be developed. Therefore, providing for managerial career planning on a selective basis is both prudent and inevitable, provided of course that the selection of candidates is not blatantly discriminatory.

Managerial career planning requires assessing the future and determining what key managerial vacancies are likely to occur at given points along the way. While somewhat less predictable in many rapidly changing industries, there is still the need for projecting likely requirements, including the impact of the chain reaction of promotions that may occur. In effect, a series of replacement tables, either formal or informal, must be developed that will identify potential candidates for anticipated vacancies. Even in those organizations where company policy or union agreement may prescribe competitive examination, there needs to be some prediction of turnover together with a clear definition of the qualifications so that opportunity for proper preparation is made available to potential candidates. Preparation activities may range from a variety of informal work assignments to a job rotation effort to informal as well as formal education and training.

It should appear quite obvious by now that, even though we are talking about managerial career planning *from the organization's perspective,* most of the activities identified will require both the cooperation and the productive input of the individual concerned. Here is where the skill of the supervisor as a coach is brought into play. This includes the determination that a compatibility exists between the plan, formal or informal, that the organization has in mind and the personal desires of the individual being considered. When the plan can be brought into focus so that it meets the needs of both the organization and the individual, the supervisor facilitating that process is performing a valuable service to both.

From the individual manager's perspective, managerial career planning begins with an identification of personal goals or career directions. Typically, this projection will change several times during a person's career and will include considerations both inside and outside of the current organization. Regardless of these changes, however, the individual manager can use objectives and results as an effective means of planning and progressing along a productive route to career growth.

The truly ambitious manager will not wait until there is a designation from someone on high to participate in a career development plan. That individual will establish a personal development plan that may encompass all of the considerations the organization might include in its own program. The principal point to remember is that very few significant career achievements occur without a plan.

In setting up one's own career development plan, the individual manager may well set certain interim goals as a test for the organization to see how serious it is in providing reasonable opportunities for advancement. If the results achieved are not consistent with personal career objectives, there is a decision junction with one of three basic plans to follow. The individual may accept "the inevitable" and go along with whatever plan has been decided by the organization; he or she may readjust and set some new objectives that may be more realistic; or there may be a decision to leave the organization for another where the opportunity to achieve desired objectives may be greater. There are variations on these three paths, of course, but essentially the next step is in one of these three alternatives. There is a fourth alternative that some managers at that point in their careers choose to follow, and that is to remain in the position and demonstrate either passive or active resistance to what was obviously poor judgment or "politics." This is not an acceptable alternative in our opinion because it is regressive in nature, whereas the other three represent positive (even if less than ideal) plans.

Managerial career planning can be pursued somewhat independently by the organization and by individual managers within the organization. While there is some benefit to be derived from this approach, the real payoff comes when the two are integrated into a similar, if not common, plan.

SUMMARY

Manager/supervisor appraisal and development is quite similar in many ways to employee appraisal and development. The differences are primarily differences in scope because of the generally broader nature of the managerial job and the fact that appraisal and development of a manager must consider at length the effect the manager has on the output of others.

There are four general areas that are a part of the appraisal and development process for a manager: unit output, self output, performance in the functions of management, and performance and development of employees. The three appraisal and development models described in Chapter 4 can be applied effectively to the job of a manager, bearing these four general areas in mind.

Managerial career planning, while related to manager development, is a specific planning effort related to long-range career goals, from the perspectives of both the organization and the individual manager. The use of objectives and results can and should be an integral part of any effort to achieve the best payoff for all concerned.

ENDNOTES

1. George L. Morrisey, *Management by Objectives and Results for Business and Industry* (Reading, Mass.: Addison-Wesley, 1977), pp. 9–10.
2. Ibid., p. 11.

6

Performance Standards and a Planned Approach to Appraisal and Development*

The words performance standards have stimulated a lot of emotional reaction virtually every time they have been introduced as a part of performance appraisal. Any truly effective organization is dependent on the establishment of mutually understood and accepted performance standards in carrying out its functions, yet the establishment of standards has been a rather slipshod process for many of us who teach and write in the field. We have tended to preach a great deal about how important standards are and that everyone ought to have them. But the extent to which we have been able to provide solid, usable guidelines for others, much less apply them realistically to ourselves, has been somewhat haphazard, to say the least.

Regardless of which appraisal model or variation we may choose to follow, the establishment of specific expectations, whether we call them standards, objectives, or something else, is an absolutely essential ingredient. As we have stressed continuously throughout this book, this has more far-reaching effects than creating the "scorecard." We see it as the pivotal part of what we refer to as "A Planned Approach to Appraisal and Development." This involves the following six steps:

1. Know what you expect.
   a. Tasks/responsibilities, key results areas, or critical performance elements
   b. Performance standards, objectives, or assignments

2. Observe job performance.

3. Compare performance expectations with results.

---

*Portions of this chapter are adapted from *Management by Objectives and Results for Business and Industry* by George L. Morrisey, Addison-Wesley Publishing Co., Reading, Mass., 1977, pages 151–158.

4. Develop plan to improve performance results.

5. Use progress or development interview to motivate employee.

6. Carry out development plans and evaluate results.

We will concentrate on the first four of these steps in this chapter with the other two covered later. Let's come back again to the use of performance standards and the problems associated with them.

There are several reasons (or excuses) we frequently give for not doing a more effective job of developing *and implementing* performance standards. Here are a few (you can undoubtedly add several others you have heard or used):

The job cannot be measured.

The work is unpredictable; it is constantly changing.

Standards are too restrictive; they stifle innovation.

Standards tend to measure the wrong things.

Standards can be easily manipulated.

Development and use of standards takes more time than they are worth.

At various times, a strong case could be made in favor of any of these viewpoints. In reality, there are three primary reasons why most people tend to avoid or "pay lip service" to the use of performance standards. The first is *fear* by people who may have observed or been the victims of *negative* use of standards (for punitive purposes) or who may be reluctant to be held accountable for something they feel they may not be able to achieve. The second reason reflects two different sides of the same issue—*impatience and resistance to change*. In other words, when approaching something different, such as the use of standards, some people prefer to let the situation continue "as is" if they cannot have "instant success." The third reason why people may not do an effective job of establishing and using standards is, very simply, a lack of sufficient *knowledge and skill* to do it properly.

The first two reasons identified are largely related to personal and environmental factors which the individual manager may or may not be able to significantly influence. The last reason, *knowledge and skill,* represents an area where significant improvement is possible. While we will address the personal and environmental factors in this chapter, our primary emphasis will be on tools and techniques for acquiring the necessary knowledge and skill.

WHAT ARE STANDARDS?

In *Management by Objectives and Results for Business and Industry,* we defined a standard as "a gauge of effective performance in achieving objectives." Here we are referring to its specific application as a part of the Controlling function. Elaborating further, this implies quantification of performance factors in some manner. In some types of effort this is a relatively simple thing to do; in others, particularly those that rely heavily on creative mental activity, it becomes substantially more difficult. Yet, even subjective evaluation can be quantified. The biggest barrier to overcome in this regard is the natural reluctance of many managers to accept an imperfect unit of measurement as a standard against which to evaluate performance.

The concept of "imperfection" is vital to both the creation and the acceptance of performance standards. Standards are an imperfect method of measurement that can be affected by many variables. There is no infallible way to measure performance. However, the fact that we may have to look beyond the standards themselves periodically to assess performance and that we may have to make exceptions to the standards on occasion does not invalidate their use. The key to the effective use of standards is a recognition that human judgment can never be removed from the evaluation process. Standards help us to focus our energies on measurable factors that have a high probability of reflecting satisfactory performance.

A person's entire life—not only work life—is built around standards of one sort or another. Relative success or failure in everything we do is determined by accepted standards, whether they be school grades, sports achievement, income level, weight, or gas mileage. Standards in these categories are no more "perfect" than the performance standards we establish in our work. Still, we generally accept them and adjust our living to them until a better method of measurement comes along.

One message that should be coming through here is that the use of performance standards should be just as beneficial to the individual as to the organization, if not more so. They provide a target to shoot for and a means for tracking one's own performance. In this way, the individual knows in advance what constitutes winning performance and is able to determine where he or she stands in relation to it.

WHAT ARE SOME ADVANTAGES AND USES OF STANDARDS?

While the use of standards for performance evaluation may be one of the more obvious uses of standards, there are many potential advantages to their use. Here are a few of the more important ones:

1. Yardstick for determining the probability of reaching objectives

2. Means of measuring individual performance for purposes of:
   a. Compensation
   b. Employee development
   c. Work assignments
   d. Promotions
   e. Downgrading or disciplinary action

3. Incentive for individual improvement

4. Incentive for unit improvement

5. Incentive for innovative approaches to work performance

6. Means of *self*-measurement and correction

7. Means of interpreting the performance of others

8. Means of making realistic forecasts for:
   a. Staff-loading purposes
   b. Facility, equipment, and material needs
   c. Evaluating and making tradeoffs on objectives
   d. Costing purposes (seeking appropriations)

9. Incentive and means for continuous and consistent reevaluation of methods and results

10. Means of comparison with the performance of other organizations or units

HOW DO WE ESTABLISH PERFORMANCE STANDARDS?

Referring to the concept of "imperfection," let's remember that the prime purpose of a standard is to serve as an indicator of successful performance. Therefore, failure to meet a particular standard is nothing more than a signal that something is wrong and that some sort of corrective action may be indicated.

There are literally thousands of measurable factors that could be used as performance standards. You will have to make your own determination as to which ones will best serve your purposes. A "brainstorming" session with fellow workers may well uncover some useful factors that might otherwise be overlooked—not to mention the motivational value that comes from permitting those concerned to have a say in establishing the standards.

Here are some frequently used measurable factors that could be related to some staff operations, which can serve as thought stimulators in determining your own:

Volume of people served	Flow time
New services provided	Requests for service
New organizations served	Degree of acceptance
Promotional costs	Cost reductions
Cost per unit of service	Accuracy/neatness
Number of employees	Units of service produced/provided

Promotions	Errors, rejects
Cost per applicant processed	Turnaround time
Turnover rate	Lost-time accidents
Percent of savings	Maintenance costs
Equipment utilization	Down time
Calendar time	Percent of overtime
Ideas generated	Changes initiated
Schedule milestones	Problems/opportunities

Note that some of these examples of measurable performance factors, such as degree of acceptance, ideas generated, problems/opportunities, etc., are quite subjective, whereas others imply varying degrees of objectivity/subjectivity. The fact remains that some form of measurement can be placed on each of them, so that each can serve as an indicator of successful performance. The same applies to the thousands of other factors that can be used as measuring devices. You must decide which factors will be the best indicators of successful performance toward the achievement of your unit's objectives.

Once the measurable factors have been identified, the manager must determine the point of measurement that constitutes effective performance. This is usually expressed as one of the following: (1) *numbers* (hours, units, requests); (2) *dollars* (unit costs, maintenance costs); (3) *percentages* (overtime, errors, equipment utilization); (4) *time lapse* (flow time, setup time, turnaround time); or (5) *completion point* (milestones, acceptance, problems overcome).

The process of determining the specific point of measurement may be influenced by many considerations—past history, the manager's personal capabilities, organizational requirements or limitations, and supervisor or employee recommendations, to mention a few. By whatever means this measurement point is defined, the manager must accept the results as (1) a reasonable indicator of effective performance, and (2) a point that will provide adequate visibility in a timely fashion with a minimum expenditure of time and effort.

WHO MUST UNDERSTAND AND ACCEPT THE STANDARDS?

To be meaningful, standards must be both understood and accepted primarily by the three organizational levels most concerned with the objective-related performance—the accountable manager, his or her supervisor, and his or her employees. This is particularly critical as it relates to the employees. Let's face it! Since our employees are the ones who probably will contribute most to the achievement of our objectives, it is neither realistic nor fair to expect them to meet performance standards that they do not understand or are unwilling to accept.

The secret, if we can call it that, to bringing about understanding and acceptance on the part of employees is to get their active participation in the determination of the standards against which they will be measured. The degree of this participation will vary substantially, depending on the nature of the work, the knowledge and capabilities of the concerned employees, and the degree of sensitivity of the standards to be established. However, it is almost axiomatic that the employee's motivation toward meeting performance standards will correlate closely with the amount of involvement that individual has had in their determination. This is especially true of the more subjective measurement factors.

LEVELS AND TYPES OF STANDARDS

There are at least two distinctly different levels of standards that most supervisors will consider. The first is the *ideal,* that point to which the supervisor hopes all employees will aspire, recognizing that relatively few are likely to reach. The second is the standard of *acceptability,* that point below which performance is not considered satisfactory and which points up the need for some sort of corrective action. As an analogy, par in golf would represent the ideal and a handicap would represent acceptability.

The following three factors must be kept in mind in setting performance standards:

1. They must be realistic and achievable. If they are not within reach of the employee, even with some stretch, then either the standards or the employee should be replaced.

2. They should be set slightly above average. They should be achievable, as mentioned above, but should require some concentrated effort on the part of the employee. In other words, the employee should not be able to accomplish the task without a little extra effort.

3. They should be subject to change. Very few standards, in the sense we are using them here, remain constant. New conditions, new materials, new methods—even the experience factor—might easily require a readjustment of the standards either upward or downward. They should not be changed indiscriminately, but should be flexible enough to be revised if circumstances dictate.

Also, there is no such thing as one type of standard when a supervisor is evaluating the performance of an employee. There are at least three types of evaluation that can be applied to a greater or lesser degree in each case. Each has validity as a means of upgrading employee performance.

1. *Predetermined standards* are set for the job, irrespective of the employee performing it. These are sometimes based on the supervisor's personal performance when performing a similar job and may be unrealistic for this employee at this time. If prepared objectively, however, these standards should be valid and workable.

2. *Performance of others* in the group (individually or as an average) may serve as a standard or point of comparison. Although the relative dangers of individual comparisons are obvious, it is almost impossible to completely avoid making them. Sometimes, particularly when the average is used, comparison can be quite valid as a measuring device.

3. *The employees as individuals* can serve as their own standard, comparing where they are with where they were or should be. This takes into consideration the level of both the employee's experience and potential and could be particularly valuable for developmental purposes.

OBSERVING JOB PERFORMANCE

Once the job expectations have been established, there is a point of departure for evaluation. However, if the supervisor relies entirely on memory at the time of the evaluation, there is a strong risk of an incomplete and inaccurate analysis. There is a tendency to remember recent events more vividly than earlier ones and they may exercise a disproportionate weight in the evaluation. To ensure fair consideration at time of review, the supervisor should document relevant factors as memory joggers along the way.

A method of documentation that has proven both simple and effective is what has been called the "critical incident" method. In this, the supervisor makes and files notes of important performance incidents, both favorable and unfavorable, when they occur. They need not be elaborate and can be done in longhand, but they should provide enough information for the supervisor to be able to recall not only what happened but the conditions under which it happened. Obviously, the supervisor should point these out to the employee, for commendation or correction, at the time they occur, but they still should be used as a basis for formal evaluation as well. These could and should include such things as:

1. Records of achievement (or lack of achievement) of objectives or assignments

2. Commendations or critical comments received about the employee or her or his work

3. Specific evidences of work output

4. Spot-check observations of performance

5. Attendance reports

6. Records of any disciplinary action taken

7. Records of prior discussions related to work performance

8. Special activities or awards that may be beyond the normal work expectancy, but reflect directly or indirectly on the employee's performance

WHAT IF PERFORMANCE DOES NOT MEET THE STANDARDS ESTABLISHED?

If an employee's performance does not come up to the supervisor's expectations, the natural assumption is that the employee is failing to perform effectively. This is not necessarily a valid assumption. We should bear in mind that failure to meet a performance expectation or standard is a "red flag," nothing more, nothing less. It says, "Whoa! Stop! Tilt! Something's wrong! Let's take a look at it."

Basically, if a standard is not reached, the cause of deviation might be traced to any one or combination of three contributing factors.

1. *The employee* may very well be the key factor. Perhaps there was carelessness or negligence; perhaps the job requirements are beyond that employee's current capability; perhaps the job holds little challenge or interest; perhaps there are outside factors affecting his or her personal life—health, family, financial, legal, etc.—that are having a temporary adverse effect on performance.

2. *The supervisor* may be the real culprit, without realizing it. Maybe there was a failure to clearly identify performance expectations; maybe it was assumed that the employee understood without checking to confirm that understanding; maybe there was an unrealistic standard (e.g., too short a time period); maybe the proper tools and training were not made available.

3. *The situation* may present some circumstances that are literally beyond the employee's control (e.g., waiting for a key report from another department). There may be any number of factors that might interfere with effective employee performance either temporarily or permanently.

This discussion points out the fact that we must resist the temptation to look for a single, simple solution to an employee's failure to meet a standard. There frequently are many causes and, as supervisors, we must identify the various possibilities and then, perhaps, do some testing to determine which are the ones deserving our attention.

In order for an employee to satisfactorily meet a performance standard, three conditions affecting that employee must exist. The employee must clearly *understand* what is expected, be *capable* of performing the work, and be *willing* to do it. If any one item is lacking, there is little likelihood of success. Each of these will be examined in more detail.

In order for an employee to *understand* what is expected, there must be a clear and precise agreement *in advance* between the employee and the supervisor. As supervisors, we frequently tend to assume that a standard of performance that is perfectly clear to us is equally clear to others. Then, when an employee fails to measure up to our expectations, we reach the conclusion that the employee is either unwilling or unable to do the job correctly. In reality, the employee's perception of what is expected may be considerably different from that of the supervisor. As a simple example, if an expectation is that a telephone be answered promptly, anything over one ring might be unacceptable to the supervisor, whereas an employee might feel that it is more important to come to a convenient stopping point in whatever other work he or she may be doing (such as typing a letter), as long as the phone does not ring more than three or four times. "Answering the phone promptly" is not a standard; "answering the phone in two rings or less" *is* a standard. A standard must be measurable enough so that all concerned parties can recognize that it has or has not been achieved. It should be arrived at through mutual discussion and agreement and it should be in writing, where practical, particularly if it is to be a continuing expectation.

Whether or not an employee is *capable* of performing a task refers to both internal and external capability. Internal capability is related to the amount of knowledge and skill the employee has. If a person lacks the necessary knowledge and skill to do something, then obviously that person will be unable to meet an expected level of performance. Knowledge and skill, of course, can be acquired through study and training, if it is important that the individual be able to perform at a designated level. Internal capability represents something that is within the individual.

External capability, on the other hand, refers to factors outside the individual that affect his or her ability to perform satisfactorily. This includes such things as sufficient time to do the job (in line with other responsibilities), tools, equipment, material, and other human resources. In other words, an employee may have the necessary knowledge and skill, but if he or she has more work than can be reasonably accomplished in the time allocated or is not provided with the wherewithal and support to do the job, that employee is not *capable* of performing. The responsibility for this situation, of course, lies more with the supervisor or the organization than with the employee.

Once it is clearly determined that the employee both understands and is capable of performing satisfactorily, he or she must also be *willing* to do it. My observation has been that, if understanding and capability are present and if the particular task and the standard established are reasonable expectations for the job, willingness on the part of the employee is rarely a problem.

All three conditions, *understanding, capability,* and *willingness,* must exist if an employee is to perform up to standard. If any one is insufficient or missing, it is unlikely that the employee's performance will be satisfactory. When a person's performance is falling short, our recommendation is to check first for understanding, then for capability (both internal and external), before jumping to the conclusion that the employee is "not motivated" or unwilling.

USE OF "SUPERVISOR'S WORKSHEET—FORMULATING DEVELOPMENT PLANS"

As we identify some areas where an employee may need improvement, it is helpful to take a look at possible explanations and possible courses of action. The worksheet shown as Fig. 6.1 is an excellent way to organize your thinking in this process. This is not to imply that the supervisor should come into an interview with the employee with a carefully worked out plan to present for the employee's development. Such an approach would, in all probability, be doomed to little more than perfunctory compliance. The plan most likely to be carried out is one that evolves as a result of the discussion between the supervisor and the employee. Also, there is a direct correlation between the participation of the employee in the development of the plan and its probability of success. However, this does not mean that the supervisor should not give careful thought to possible alternative courses of action. He or she should come into the interview with some good, constructive suggestions to offer if and when the situation calls for it. Thus, we refer to this as a "worksheet" and not a "form." (A form is usually viewed as something the completion of which is an end in itself, whereas a worksheet is a tool that is a means to the end.)

It is important to note that we are identifying *possible* explanations and *possible* courses of action. They may or may not be valid. Using the worksheet, however, forces us to look beyond what may be the most obvious (but not necessarily the most accurate) direction to follow. If both the supervisor and the employee can agree up front on the improvement need to be addressed, then it may be appropriate for each to complete a worksheet independently and then compare answers. (You may reproduce this worksheet for your own use, provided the credit shown at the bottom of the page is included.) Figures 6.2 through 6.5 are hypothetical examples of the use of this worksheet.

WORKSHEET EXAMPLES

Systems Specialist
Mary Allen is a Systems Specialist in a large organization. She has established an excellent reputation in the two years she has been in the position, and is well liked and respected by most of the people in the departments with whom she

Fig. 6.1 Supervisor's worksheet.

SUPERVISOR'S WORKSHEET

FORMULATING DEVELOPMENT PLANS

Improvement Need:_____   Employee:_____

_____   Supervisor:_____

Growth Goal:_____   Dept.:_____

_____   Date:_____

POSSIBLE EXPLANATIONS	POSSIBLE COURSES OF ACTION
Within the individual	For the individual
Within the supervisor	For the supervisor
Within the situation or job itself	To change the situation or job itself

From *Performance Appraisals in Business and Industry* by George L. Morrisey, Addison-Wesley Publishing Co., Reading, Mass. 1983. Permission to reproduce granted.

has worked. Her supervisor, Bob Muncrief, is generally pleased with her professionalism and the reception she receives in her assignments. His primary concern about her performance is that she tends to take 20 to 30 percent more time to complete her assignments than do most of her colleagues. Bob has observed Mary involved in extensive discussions with individual employees, apparently over personal matters, while on assignment. When asked about this, Mary replied that these employees have no one else with whom they can discuss their personal problems. She feels that helping these individuals goes a long way toward increasing her credibility and that she can do a more effective job on her assignments as a result. While sympathetic to her position, Bob feels that the demand for services from their department is such that Mary must reduce the time she is currently spending on some of her assignments so that she will be available more often to help meet that demand. He feels that an appropriate growth goal or standard on which he would like to reach agreement with Mary is for her to have specific task objectives for each assignment, approved by him, with an action plan, including time allocations. In his judgment, this should enable her to focus her efforts more specifically and, as a result, complete her assignments in a shorter time period. In preparation for his meeting with Mary, Bob has completed the worksheet shown in Fig. 6.2 so that he can discuss various alternatives with her.

Placement Specialist
Ralph Armbruster is a Placement Specialist in the Employment Services Department. In line with accepted practice in that department, Ralph is assigned to three line departments as the one responsible for filling all employment vacancies there. Ralph's supervisor, Ruth Sylvester, believes that the assigned Placement Specialist should be dealing directly with the line managers in the using departments so that he or she can be more responsive to their employment needs. In Ralph's situation, Ruth feels that the relations with line managers leave a lot to be desired. The managers tend to call her directly to discuss their needs rather than dealing with Ralph. Ralph's reaction is that these managers are calling on trivial matters and that if they would just leave him alone he could get his job done more effectively. Ruth feels that for Ralph to perform his job satisfactorily they must reach agreement on a growth goal or standard which will result in direct communication between Ralph and the line managers he is serving *without* a requirement for regular intervention on her part as the supervisor. Figure 6.3 shows the worksheet Ruth has completed in preparation for her discussion with Ralph.

Project Planner
Tom Williams is a Project Planner with a responsibility for analyzing data submitted from field operations, projecting trends, and preparing forecast charts on the need for technical services. Recently, through a departmental consolidation, he has had to assume the responsibility for generating some reg-

Fig. 6.2 Sample worksheet.

SUPERVISOR'S WORKSHEET

FORMULATING DEVELOPMENT PLANS

Improvement Need: Reduce time
spent on assignments.

Growth Goal: Have approved
objectives for each assignment with
action plan, including time
allocations.

Employee: Mary Allen, Systems
Specialist

Supervisor: Bob Muncrief

Dept.: Systems

Date: November 1

POSSIBLE EXPLANATIONS	POSSIBLE COURSES OF ACTION
Within the individual	**For the individual**
1. May lack skill in developing task objectives.	1. Study, training, and/or counseling may need to be provided.
2. May lack discipline in following plan.	2. Establish milestones, including review with supervisor.
3. May put desire to provide personal counseling above task.	3. Commit to placing completion of task objectives first.
Within the supervisor	**For the supervisor**
1. No clear agreement on task objectives and time allocations.	1. Establish this as a requirement with mutual agreement in advance.
2. No clear priorities on importance of various potential assignments.	2. In consultation with affected employees, establish system for setting priorities.
3. May not be sensitive to some important unsatisfied needs in the organization.	3. Establish plan for making personal visits to using departments to assess needs.
Within the situation or job itself	**To change the situation or job itself**
1. May be need for increased personal counseling services.	1. If so, evaluate and make recommendations to higher management on a plan to satisfy that need.
2. Line managers may not understand how to use services.	2. Establish guidelines with and for line managers and counsel employee on interpretation.
3. Demand for services may exceed supply capability.	3. Make recommendations to higher management on priorities and/or increasing capability to meet demand.

Fig. 6.3 Sample worksheet.

SUPERVISOR'S WORKSHEET

FORMULATING DEVELOPMENT PLANS

Improvement Need: Relations with
line managers in using departments.

Growth Goal: Direct communication
with line managers without
requirement for supervisor's
intervention.

Employee: Ralph Armbruster,
Placement Spec.

Supervisor: Ruth Sylvester

Dept.: Employment Services

Date: February 1

POSSIBLE EXPLANATIONS	POSSIBLE COURSES OF ACTION
Within the individual	**For the individual**
1. May not understand true nature of work in using departments.	1. Develop plan for increasing familiarity with work in the using departments.
2. May not understand or accept line managers as "customers."	2. Training or counseling on the role of the internal consultant.
3. May lack sufficient skill in interpersonal communications.	3. Study, training, or counseling on interpersonal communications skills.
Within the supervisor	**For the supervisor**
1. No clear agreement on employee's role with line managers.	1. Establish mutually agreed-to written understanding on employee's role.
2. Insufficient progress reviews with employee.	2. Schedule once a month initially.
3. Inefficient scheduling to meet workload requirements.	3. Reevaluate scheduling methods to make better use of employee's time.
Within the situation or job itself	**To change the situation or job itself**
1. Distance of using departments from Employment office.	1. Arrange employee's schedule to permit more frequent visits to using departments.
2. Line managers may not provide sufficient information or may have unrealistic expectations.	2. Establish guidelines with and for line managers and counsel employee on their interpretation.
3. Qualified applicants in some classifications may be in short supply.	3. Reevaluate recruiting methods and modify as needed; continually interpret situation to line managers, seeking their understanding and cooperation.

ular monthly status reports on specific projects in work. He has been consistently late in turning these in since that has been added to his duties. Tom's supervisor, Joe Martin, feels that this is due to two primary reasons—poor self-organizational practices on Tom's part and a continuing friction between Tom and members of the clerical pool on whom he must rely for typing support. Joe feels that Tom may be using the schedule slippages as a form of protest for the additional workload but that, through more efficient organization and by improving his relations with the clerical pool, Tom should be able to meet the requirement of getting the reports in on time. In order to prepare for his meeting with Tom, Joe has completed the worksheet as shown in Fig. 6.4.

Supervisor of Technical Services
Marilyn McGregor is the Supervisor of Technical Services described in Chapter 5. As was pointed out there, she has outstanding technical skills and still performs a significant amount of technical work in addition to her supervisory responsibilities. While, theoretically, her job is supposed to be half technical and half supervisory, she actually spends about 60 percent of her time on technical tasks with the majority of her "supervisory" time devoted to attending meetings and completing paperwork. Her supervisor, Ardis Allen, feels that Marilyn needs to delegate at least half of the technical work she is currently handling so that she can devote more time to improving productivity and to the development of her employees. Ardis has used the worksheet as shown in Fig. 6.5 to collect some thoughts prior to a meeting with Marilyn.

We will not speculate on the outcome of these four meetings between supervisors and employees. However, by going through the kind of analysis indicated on the worksheets and by identifying some reasonable standards toward which to direct their efforts, the supervisors will be in a much better position to help bring about a mutual agreement on performance improvement.

SUMMARY

People tend to avoid or "pay lip service" to the use of performance standards for three primary reasons: (1) fear of negative consequences, (2) impatience and resistance to change, and (3) lack of requisite knowledge and skill. The greatest amount of visible improvement can be brought about in addressing the third reason. Furthermore, proper attention there can significantly affect the other two as well.

A standard is "a gauge of effective performance in achieving objectives" and has a wide variety of uses, including a means of measuring individual performance. It is an "imperfect" method of measurement that requires the exercise of good judgment in its use. Furthermore, the use of standards must be just as beneficial to the individual as to the organization or they will prove relatively ineffective. There is a high correlation between the degree of acceptance of standards and the amount of involvement in their determination by those affected by them.

Fig. 6.4 Sample worksheet.

SUPERVISOR'S WORKSHEET

FORMULATING DEVELOPMENT PLANS

Improvement Need: Reduce or
eliminate lateness of written
reports.

Growth Goal: Reports will be in on
time.

Employee: Tom Williams, Project
Planner

Supervisor: Joe Martin

Dept.: Planning

Date: June 1

POSSIBLE EXPLANATIONS	POSSIBLE COURSES OF ACTION
Within the individual	**For the individual**
1. Poor self-organizational practices.	1. Review suggested plans for organizing one's work and adopt one suitable.
2. Lack of effective cooperation with clerical pool.	2. Develop more patience and understanding in dealing with clerical staff.
3. Poor dictating practices.	3. Develop a key-word outline prior to dictating.
4. Resistance to change; e.g., taking on additional duties (written reports).	4. Develop better understanding of reasons for work consolidation and importance of reports.
Within the supervisor	**For the supervisor**
1. Have not emphasized the importance of timely written reports sufficiently.	1. Discuss in more depth with Tom and emphasize his responsibility.
2. Failed to give adequate recognition for work done well and for extra effort required for additional duties.	2. Emphasize his fine job on forecast charts and his pinpoint accuracy; point out director's comments.
3. Failed to establish system for determining priorities on clerical work.	3. Establish priority-determination system with provision for conflict resolution by supervisor.
Within the situation or job itself	**To change the situation or job itself**
1. Too much work for one employee.	1. Examine workloads for possible shifting of responsibilities.
2. Clerical staff may be playing favorites.	2. (See #3 under supervisor.)
3. Delays in receiving inputs required to complete report.	3. Investigate and eliminate any bottlenecks in getting necessary information to Tom.

Fig. 6.5 Sample worksheet.

SUPERVISOR'S WORKSHEET

FORMULATING DEVELOPMENT PLANS

Improvement Need: Increase time
allocated to supervisory
responsibilities.

Growth Goal: Delegate minimum ½ of
technical tasks to employees within
nine months.

Employee: Marilyn McGregor,
Supervisor

Supervisor: Ardis Allen

Dept.: Technical Operations

Date: June 1

POSSIBLE EXPLANATIONS	POSSIBLE COURSES OF ACTION
Within the individual	**For the individual**
1. Enjoys technical work and reluctant to give it up.	1. Clarify responsibilities and establish priorities.
2. Insecure in supervisory role.	2. Analyze job elements for relative importance.
3. Lacks skills in training employees.	3. Training/coaching in skill development.
Within the supervisor	**For the supervisor**
1. Priorities not clearly established.	1. Discuss and clarify.
2. Lack of encouragement and support for role as supervisor.	2. Increase counseling time with Marilyn.
3. Skill training not provided.	3. Arrange for appropriate training.
Within the situation or job itself	**To change the situation or job itself**
1. Excessive workload.	1. Assess, streamline, and realign.
2. Inadequately trained employees.	2. Provide formal and informal training as needed.
3. Pressure from outside users.	3. Supervisor serve as buffer between Marilyn and outside users.

To be meaningful, standards must be *realistic and achievable,* should be set *slightly above average,* and should be *subject to change* as needed. Three types of evaluation are used to establish standards: (1) *predetermined standards,* (2) comparison with the *performance of others,* and (3) comparison with the *employee's own performance.*

Failure of an employee to meet a standard could be caused by any or all of three different contributing factors: (1) *the employee's performance,* (2) *the supervisor's performance,* and (3) *the situation or job itself.* Each must be examined before jumping to what might be the most obvious (but not necessarily the most appropriate) conclusion. For an employee to satisfactorily meet a performance standard, three conditions must exist. The employee must clearly *understand* what is expected, be *capable* of performing the work, and be *willing* to do it. All three must be present or there is little likelihood of success.

Properly used, the establishment and implementation of performance standards as a part of a planned approach to appraising and developing employees can be one of the most positive and powerful forces in the effective management of an organization.

7

The Case for Employee Development

There are two principal goals of any effective employee development effort. The first and foremost is to improve the performance of employees *in their present jobs.* This is the payoff, the place where employee development should provide its biggest return. In fact, any stated goal that is placed before this should be cause for real concern on the part of management people. Employee development, despite its lofty title, is *not* a philanthropic activity. It must provide some immediate as well as long-term benefit.

The second goal, preparing the employee for possible *future opportunities,* is a bit more tenuous than the first. On the one hand, it is a natural fall-out of the first, building on the basic philosophy that the most effective way for the employee to be promoted is to do the best possible job in the present position. However, we would be shortsighted if we failed to recognize that the scope of the present position may not provide the opportunity for all the developmental activities needed in preparation for that future position. Therefore, the supervisor must make an analysis of the employee's potential as it relates to the organization's present and future human resource needs. Furthermore, for it to be useful, this analysis must be documented in some form that reflects reasonable objectivity.

Realistically, any approach to employee development is going to represent a significant cost (perhaps, more appropriately, an investment) for all of the principal parties concerned—the organization, the immediate supervisor, and the individual employee. In Chapter 1, we identified several potential benefits (both "loss avoided" and "value added") for each of these three groups. Obviously, the vast majority of those benefits will come far more from the *development* part of the process than from the appraisal or scorekeeping part.

Furthermore, in the competitive world of today, employee development is becoming a matter of survival. The only way an organization can expect to operate effectively and efficiently over an extended period of time is with the continued upgrading of the capabilities of its work force. Highly skilled people are rarely available on the labor market. Even if you had the freedom to try it, the old philosophy of "hire, try'er, fire, and rehire" just would not accomplish the job. A well-planned approach to employee development is the most practical alternative solution.

WHO? THE RESPONSIBILITY FOR EMPLOYEE DEVELOPMENT

"Nobody ever developed me!" "I haven't got the time!" "Good employees, like the cream in fresh milk, always rise to the top!" "Why should I develop people for someone else?"

Do these sound familiar? They are among the more frequent comments made by supervisors on the subject of employee development. To a certain degree, there is some truth in each, but we cannot use them as excuses for not doing our supervisory jobs. To be sure, the employee has the prime responsibility for his or her own development; however, it is both a rare individual and a rare set of circumstances that will lead to an employee being completely self-contained in the development process. An employee can be given substantial assistance in development from a variety of sources, and considering what each has at stake, there are very real responsibilities that can be assigned to top management; the personnel, management development, or other related staff organizations; the immediate supervisor; and the individual employee.

Top Management

Top management's responsibility begins with a philosophy of support and direction. As stated earlier, the key management team must be firmly committed to the return-on-investment value of an effective appraisal and development effort and must make it known to the rest of management that a positive and continuing effort in this direction will be one of the critical activities by which they, as managers, will be evaluated. Anything less than this will result in a relatively sterile effort with little long-range benefit. More specifically, top management's responsibility is to:

1. Provide the policies and procedures required to implement the effort

2. Provide the administrative controls to ensure compliance

3. Provide the budget (including allowance for time off from work when necessary) for the development requirements and opportunities identified

4. Demonstrate its interest by action *and example*

5. Provide the proper climate whereby development can be encouraged

6. Demonstrate to everyone, including other top management people, that it is important to continuously work on self-improvement and that such effort is being evaluated

The Personnel, Management Development, or Other Related Staff Organization

Herein lies the responsibility to provide line management with as much assistance as possible to ensure effective application of the appraisal and development process. The importance of the word *assistance* cannot be overemphasized here. Actions related to appraisal and development are almost exclusively the province of line management. In those organizations where appraisal and development is seen as another "Personnel program," it should not be surprising to discover that the vast majority of managers in the organization feel very little sense of commitment to making it work more than just superficially. No staff organization should usurp the functions of line management. Its responsibility is to do everything possible to help line management do its employee development job better. The Personnel Department will not relieve the manager of the responsibility for employee development, but will help make it more meaningful by:

1. Stimulating interest in appraisal and development

2. Training and coaching managers in carrying out their appraisal and development responsibilities

3. Administering and interpreting related policies and procedures

4. Following up and reporting organizational activities in employee development

5. Providing the means for satisfying training and educational needs for employees as identified through development plans

The Immediate Supervisor

More direct responsibility lies with the immediate supervisor than either of the first two categories mentioned, even though the supervisor cannot operate with any significant degree of effectiveness without their support. The supervisor is in the best position of anyone (other than the employee) to both evaluate and motivate the employee; conversely, he or she is in the best position to bring the appraisal and development effort to a screeching halt through resistance to the process or any part of it. Supervisory responsibility toward employees can be fulfilled by doing any or all of the following when appropriate:

1. Encouraging the employee in self-development

2. Training the employee to handle current work assignments more efficiently

3. Demonstrating active interest in employee development

4. Determining performance expectations or, when possible, assisting employees in determining realistic expectations of their own

5. Making certain that there is a mutual understanding of expectations

6. Operating the work unit in a way that is conducive to the growth and development of people

7. Constructively observing and measuring the performance of employees

8. Assessing the strengths and development needs of employees

9. Effectively planning for employee appraisal and development discussions

10. Holding effective, constructive employee appraisal and development discussions that have been planned to assist and encourage employees to develop their skills and abilities

11. Assisting the employee in making development plans

12. Continually reassessing the scope of the employee's job to make certain it provides ample growth opportunities

13. Following up and carrying out appropriate supervisory responsibilities in connection with any development plans that have been made

14. Investigating and, when appropriate, encouraging the employee to consider transfer or promotional opportunities outside the work unit (or even the organization), if none is available within

15. Identifying and making known to higher supervision those employees qualified for greater responsibility

The Individual Employee

The individual employee has perhaps the most to gain or lose from the employee development process, so conceivably the primary effort should rest there. There is no argument to the oft-quoted statement that people cannot be developed, but must develop themselves. The only problem with that statement is that many supervisors use it as a "cop out" to justify their failures in this regard. While the individual is the one who ultimately must be responsible for his or her own development, it is the supervisor who makes most of the opportunities available. Supervisors beware—*anyone proceeding with self-*

development without any assistance or interest from supervision is probably preparing for a better job in a different organization!

Recognizing the triple role of individual, member of a work group, and organizational employee (each of which will be in conflict with the others on occasion), the employee can fulfill responsibilities in the development process by:

1. Performing as effectively and efficiently as possible in current assignments

2. Demonstrating interest in her or his own development and its relation to the goals of the organization and the work unit

3. Seeking out opportunities for development which will benefit all concerned

4. Taking the responsibility for following through on personal development within the prescribed plan

5. Taking advantage of available development opportunities

6. Allocating the time (frequently personal time) and effort required to participate in education and training activities

7. Exercising self-discipline in on-the-job application

8. Communicating openly and regularly with supervisor, peers, and (where applicable) direct reports on development matters that affect them

WHEN? THE IMPORTANCE OF TIMING

Employee development cannot be effectively regimented. It can and should be most effective when directly related to events that occur as part of the employee's regular work assignments. Realistically though, most supervisors need some sort of system both as an aid to and a reminder of what is expected of them in the area of employee development.

A regimented approach of conducting performance appraisals on a regularly scheduled basis—whether it be once a year, twice a year, once a quarter, or once a month—creates an understandable resistance in many supervisors. Yet we cannot help but wonder how many appraisal interviews would ever take place at all without a prescribed deadline. There are supervisors who, in all sincerity, will say, "I am in continuous informal discussion of performance with all of my people. My employees know where they stand and where they are going. Nothing would be gained by having a formal review as well." Experience has shown, however, that the vast majority of the employees of these same supervisors would disagree, expressing the desire for a better understanding with their supervisors on their total performance.

Consequently, there appears to be a need for regularly scheduled appraisal and development interviews to provide an opportunity for both the supervisor and the employee to step back and take a look at the whole forest rather than a few individual trees. The continuous informal discussions usually are quite specific in nature and are a necessary prerequisite, but not a replacement, for the periodic formal review. The frequency requirement for such reviews will vary widely. It is conceivable that there may be some long-time, highly professional employees who are largely self-starters from whom a single formal review a year may be sufficient. At the same time, there may be some newer, less experienced employees for whom a formal review at least once a month is desirable. For most individuals, a quarterly review seems to be sufficient to satisfy the needs of both parties concerned without an excessive investment of either time or effort.

This discussion would lead one to believe that the interview, formal or informal, is at the heart of an employee development effort. It is! The interview is the means by which attention is focused and agreement is reached on a mutually beneficial course of action. (The interview will be discussed specifically in Chapter 9.) The interview is only the starting point, however. Timing is an equally important factor in the activities that will be a part of the employee's development plan.

WHAT? PRACTICAL EMPLOYEE DEVELOPMENT ACTIVITIES

An individual's plan for increasing knowledge and skill might include (but not be restricted to) such activities as the following:

Expanded responsibilities.   This is probably the development technique most frequently used, in which the employee is assigned additional responsibilities that provide the kind of experience needed. More specifically, this involves job enrichment or vertical enlargement of the job, creating opportunities for the individual to use higher-level skills and to influence the organization upward.

Job rotation.   This can be a formal plan with the employee being assigned to different jobs for a prescribed period—or to an informal cross-training program—as a means of learning the basics of other jobs in the organization.

"Assistant to" positions.   Here a promising young employee serves as a staff assistant to a higher-level manager for a limited period of time to provide the executive perspective and a broader point of view of organizational operations.

Staff development meetings.   Work unit members meet together on a regular basis for the express purpose of discussing facets of their jobs as a means of broadening the knowledge and understanding of the entire staff (as compared to the other, and necessary, type of staff meeting that deals with operational considerations and calendar clearances).

Problem-solving conferences.   A conference is called to make use of the creative thinking of employees through brainstorming or some other problem-solving technique to achieve a breakthrough on some organizational or unit plan or problem.

Special assignments.   Not to be overlooked, special job assignments are frequently one of the best ways of developing an employee and determining what that person can do. These could include anything from preparing a department newsletter to revising a procedure to investigating a new type of service that should be offered.

In-house training programs.   These may cover anything from organizational policy and procedure to any general or specialized training programs that can be conducted effectively by organizational personnel.

Contracted training programs.   A particular training expertise may not be readily available within the organization. Therefore, an outside specialist may be brought in to conduct a program, thus satisfying an organizational development need with a relatively modest short-term investment.

Outside short courses and seminars.   Selective attendance at specialized one-day to one-week programs sponsored by educational institutions, professional associations, or private firms provides the opportunity to meet and exchange views with people in similar positions from other organizations in addition to benefiting from the content of the program itself.

College or university degree and certificate programs.   Many educational institutions offer planned part-time programs ranging from a six- to eight-course package leading to a certificate in such things as business management or systems technology to a full graduate school degree.

Advanced management programs at colleges and universities.   These include in-residence programs ranging from a few weeks to a full year or more at major institutions (Harvard, MIT, and Stanford are three of the more prominent ones) featuring the total executive spectrum presented by prominent educators. Part-time programs of a similar nature are offered by several colleges and universities throughout the country, many with excellent reputations. Participation is usually limited to senior management personnel.

Correspondence schools.   Although not as popular as they once were, correspondence courses can be a very effective means whereby an individual can broaden capabilities on a more flexible schedule than is required in a regular school. Rigorous self-discipline is a must, however. Student mortality rates are high.

Outside meetings and conferences.   Participation in professional societies and management groups and attendance at conferences and workshops sponsored by such groups is another excellent means of broadening one's knowledge and capabilities.

Audiocassette programs.   This is perhaps the fastest growing self-instructional method. There are many programs available, ranging from highly technical subjects to foreign languages to management techniques to personal development to sales or persuasive techniques to motivational and inspirational speeches. Making use of what otherwise might be nonproductive time (driving, commuter transportation—using an earphone, lunch and break periods, off-hours—rather than watching TV), *repeatedly* playing cassettes takes advantage of the learning principle of *spaced repetition.* By hearing the same message several times, it gets "programmed" into the thinking of an individual and is a relatively painless way of learning. Cassette programs also are used quite frequently as a resource for small group learning sessions. Many organizations are using audiocassette programs to supplement their employee development efforts by partially subsidizing their purchase by employees, by distributing them (particularly with decentralized operations) with prescribed assignments, or by making them available through a lending library.

Multimedia and programmed instruction materials.   An increasing amount of educational material (some of very high quality, some absolutely worthless) is being made available for use in such media as videotape, videodisc, films, slides and filmstrips, programmed texts, so-called teaching machines, case study materials, management games, and others that can be used in a self-teaching approach or with an instructor. Remember, it is the content of the program, not the device it uses, that determines the value to the individual and to the organization. Have a subject expert review any such program before investing in it.

Computer-assisted instruction.   Another form of multimedia education, the use of the computer, is now coming into its own and will become an even stronger teaching tool in the years to come. The availability of low-cost home computers, as well as adaptations to many of the popular home video games, places this learning medium within the reach of almost everyone. Once again, the key is in the software or content of the program, not in the equipment. Many organizations have set aside learning centers where employees can go, either on their own or as a part of a group, to extend their education through this and other media.

Distribution of reading matter.   This may include circulation of books, selected articles, government periodicals, journals, abstracts or digests of current literature, etc.

Any one or any combination of these activities might be just what is needed to assure the satisfactory development of any given individual. However, none is designed to relieve the immediate supervisor of responsibility in this regard. The degree of value the individual and the organization will derive from participation in any of them will be in direct correlation with the amount of interest shown by the supervisor. If an employee's participation in any of these activities is specifically and regularly reviewed with her or his supervisor, particularly so far as whatever may be learned can be applied on the job, the subsequent learning and development by the individual will be increased many-fold.

SUMMARY

Employee development, like motherhood and patriotism, is good and should be a part of any organization's management concerns. However, it must be examined in light of the benefit to be derived by the organization, the individual employee, and the immediate supervisor, and not pursued for its own sake. Employee development represents a significant investment for all concerned and any related activities should be evaluated accordingly, on the basis of objectives and *results*. With a planned approach that reasonably assures achievement of objectives that are compatible with all concerned, employee development should receive prime attention as one of the most valuable management tools available.

8

Bringing About Favorable
Behavior Change*

As we pointed out in Chapter 1, there are discrete skills in three primary areas—performance measurement criteria, interpersonal communications, and documentation—which a supervisor must develop in order to become effective in the use of performance appraisals. Thus far in this book, we have spent most of our effort in dealing with performance measurement criteria, and somewhat more indirectly with documentation. However, without the requisite communication skills, the other two become almost academic. Therefore, the next two chapters will be devoted to improving interpersonal communications, particularly as related to what we shall refer to as the Development Interview. Before we get into a specific discussion of that, however, we need to examine some of the critical interpersonal relationships that exist between the supervisor and the individual employee.

The purpose of any development interview is reasonably clear. It is designed to bring about performance improvement (everyone can "improve," even the star performers) through joint understanding and commitment to the more effective accomplishment of mutually agreed-upon objectives. This may consist mainly of a communication process that will clarify, reinforce, or reinsure matters already reasonably understood by both parties. In many cases, if not most, however, it involves some sort of change on the part of the employee or the supervisor, or within the organizational system—sometimes all three. While we recognize that the need for change in the supervisor or the system may be of greatest importance, we will make the assumption, for our discussion in this chapter, that there is a need to bring about favorable behavior change in the employee.

---

*Some of the concepts included here were adapted from Harold J. Leavitt, *Managerial Psychology,* 4th ed. (Chicago: The University of Chicago Press, 1978).

So that we do not get confused over the psychological implications of the word *behavior,* we are using it in its simplest form. (Funk and Wagnall's: "Manner of conducting oneself; demeanor, deportment.") More specifically, we are concerned with a situation in which we want an employee to *perform* in a manner that is fundamentally different from his or her normal behavior pattern (as opposed to the simple following of directions). For example, an employee may cause friction because of an habitual manner of communicating with others. Since this is probably an ingrained part of that person's normal behavior, giving instructions on how to communicate differently is not likely to bring about any significant change.

The concept of behavior change also implies that the ensuing action will now become natural and continuing. Otherwise, the best we can hope for is *compliance.* For example, we might have a salaried employee who is habitually late in getting to work. We could, in effect, order that individual to get to work on time (with the alternative of some disciplinary action). The employee may *comply* in view of the potential consequences. However, there is likely to be considerable resentment; the employee might possibly quit; it might result in a negative attitude toward the job in general; or it probably will require a periodic reinforcement as compliance has a fairly short life span. On the other hand, if the employee accepts it as her or his responsibility to get in on time (because it is personally advantageous), and it subsequently becomes a natural habit pattern, we can call it *behavior change.* Normally, behavior change is required when there is a habit pattern or an *emotional* block that interferes with the employee performing in the expected manner. If the block is largely intellectual (lack of information, knowledge, or understanding), then a straightforward giving of directions should suffice. For example, giving of directions should take care of a routine work assignment, whereas a radical departure from the routine may require "behavior change."

WHAT MUST BE CONSIDERED?

If the supervisor has reached the conclusion that "behavior change" on the part of the employee seems indicated, then there are three factors that must be recognized and taken into consideration.

1. Examine the changer's (supervisor's) motives.   Why does the supervisor want the employee to change? Is there a good and valid reason for the change that will lead to the better accomplishment of the organization's, the unit's, and/or the employee's objectives? Or is it ego-satisfaction for the supervisor? ("I want it done my way" because it's "my way," not because it's better.) Will the change merely relieve a short-term pressure at the possible expense of a long-term objective (for example, a broadened capability in the employee)?

2. The changee (employee) is in control.   The supervisor cannot *make* anyone change. It is possible to strongly influence the situation, but the employee is the only one who can do the changing. Somehow, the employee must reach the conclusion that it is advantageous to make the change. If forced to make a change that is seen as undesirable, there are always the alternatives of quitting, going over the supervisor's head (if the demand is unreasonable), or, as is more likely, finding some less obvious way of evading, avoiding, or retaliating against any outwardly-imposed change.

3. Change is uncomfortable.   If you think back on any significant change that you have made, even one that was obviously to your benefit (promotion, new job, moving to a new location), you may recall that it was nearly always accompanied by a feeling of discomfort and uneasiness. While you had convinced yourself intellectually that this change was good, your emotional reaction still expressed some doubt. This was largely the result of a human being's normal fear of the unknown. At least your former situation was reasonably comfortable because you knew what was required and that you had the ability to meet those requirements. There are some untried areas in the new situation which may be less comfortable, at least initially, than the old rut. As another example, recall the last time you proposed an operational change to all of your employees that would obviously save both time and effort on the part of everyone. Did they accept it wholeheartedly and move enthusiastically to put it into effect? In all probability, you encountered some rather strong resistance to it for no apparent reason other than it was different, a change. This is not to imply that we should avoid change because of this factor. We cannot afford not to change when change is indicated. It does imply, however, that the discomfort factor is a very real thing and must be taken into consideration when any significant change is being approached. In fact, a lack of evidence of discomfort on the part of the changee may be a good indicator that true change is not taking place.

The employee's intellectual acceptance of the need to make a change will not in itself bring the change about. The supervisor who naively accepts such agreement at the conclusion of an interview as evidence of commitment to effective change will, in all likelihood, have to discuss the same requirement for change at the next development interview with the same employee. Such agreement for change will require a fairly intensive follow-up and reinforcement if it is to be effectively implemented.

AN APPROACH TO BEHAVIOR CHANGE

With these three factors in mind, let's examine an approach to behavior change as illustrated in the schematic diagram in Fig. 8.1. The two people most concerned, the supervisor and the employee, have specific roles to play in the process which flows logically in five successive steps.

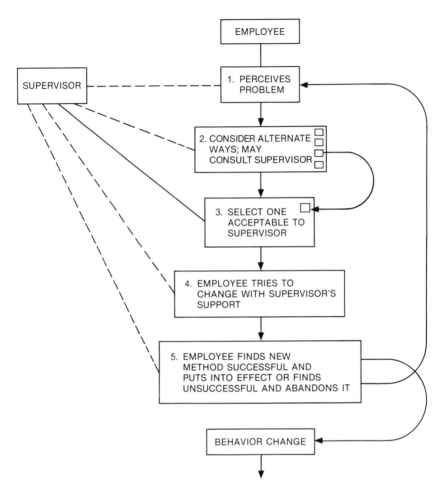

Fig. 8.1 Behavior change model.

Perception of Problem. The first and by far the most important step is perception of the problem *by the employee.* The employee must see that there is a problem and, furthermore, that it is his or her problem, one over which there is some control. (For our purposes here, *problem* is being interpreted as that form of behavior that needs to be changed for the mutual benefit of those concerned and does not necessarily imply "bad" behavior.)

Why do people change? People change when they perceive that their present behavior will no longer lead them to a result that is personally beneficial. This may come as a result of frustration caused by an externally-imposed block (a new system, a new supervisor, a change in responsibilities, etc.) or because a different way of doing something appears to have some real advantages. At any rate, the conclusion the individual reaches is that what was satisfactory behavior on her or his part in the past is not any longer.

Basically, perception of the problem means that, somehow, the employee must become dissatisfied with present behavior to the point that she or he will recognize the need for a change.

The supervisor's role, as identified in the diagram, is on a dotted-line relationship to this first step. There may or may not be a contribution the supervisor can make to the perception of the problem. It is possible for the employee to reach this step without any direct outside help. However, in real life, it is more likely that the supervisor will precipitate some action that will help the employee become dissatisfied with present behavior. What are some of these possible supervisory actions?

1. Simply assert that a problem exists, if done in a nonthreatening manner.

2. Ask the employee's opinion on how to solve a similar problem.

3. Ask the employee what seems to be interfering with the accomplishment of a recognized objective and exploring it until the real problem is identified.

4. Determine the employee's personal goals (wage increase, promotion, new learning opportunities, more challenging assignments) and identify the change with the more effective realization of these goals.

5. Place the employee into a close working relationship with someone who has the kind of work habits you would like the employee to acquire with the expectation that the employee will recognize the need for change through observation.

6. Give the employee an assignment that makes personal inadequacy quite apparent, such as increasing responsibility or giving a difficult assignment. Examples of the latter could be: training another employee in a specific job duty, having the employee work with another employee with whom there have been communication problems, or sending the employee to meetings or on coordination assignments with people who are outspoken in their criticism of such behavior.

None of these approaches is universally applicable, but each can be an effective means of helping an employee to recognize a problem and the requirement for change if it is appropriate to the individual situation. Furthermore, nearly any of them is likely to be more effective than either of the most frequently used methods—suddenly confronting the employee with the problem (at one extreme) or avoiding it and hoping it will take care of itself (at the other).

By whatever means it is reached, the achievement of this first plateau —the perception of the problem by the employee—is absolutely essential to the process of bringing about favorable behavior change. Without it, the remaining steps would be meaningless exercises because the best the supervisor could hope for would be *compliance* with his or her desires. Assuming the successful attainment of this first plateau, let's continue with the process.

Consideration of Alternative Ways.   If current behavior becomes less than satisfactory personally, the employee must examine other methods of dealing with the situation; for instance, acquiring other habit or behavior patterns that might provide more acceptable solutions. The supervisor's role again is on a dotted line in that it may be appropriate to offer some suggestions on alternate ways or the employee may develop them independently.

Selection of One Acceptable to the Supervisor.   This is the only solid-line in the entire process. Whatever method the employee selects must be acceptable to the supervisor if it is to be applied to a job-related activity. It does not necessarily have to be the ideal approach, or the one that the supervisor would most like to see used, but it does have to be at least an acceptable compromise. The supervisor has to see it as one that could logically lead to the necessary behavior change without seriously impairing normal on-the-job operations. For example, attending school a full day each week for an extended period might not be practical from an operations standpoint even though it might result in the desired behavior change.

Attempt to Change with Supervisor's Support.   Once the employee has decided on a course of action, there must be a try-out period to determine whether it will really work. Even though the relationship to the supervisor is on a dotted line in this step, it is probably the strongest such line in the entire process. Recognizing the point made earlier about change being uncomfortable, the supervisor must realize that this trial period is a crucial one and will, in all probability, require the supervisor's strong support if the employee is to make the transition effectively. It may mean that the employee's production will drop off during this transition period and that the supervisor will have to relieve her or him of some responsibilities temporarily. It doubtless will require more frequent checks with the employee both to determine progress and to offer needed encouragement.

Determination of Direction.   At this point, the employee must make a decision either to accept the new method and put it into effect, in which case it becomes a part of normal behavior and behavior change takes place, or to reject it because it is unsuccessful and to return to Step 1, *Perception of problem,* starting the process again.

This entire process can be completed in a matter of a few minutes or it may take several months, depending on the complexity of the problem and the individuals involved. The significant point that this diagram should illustrate is that for effective behavior change to occur, the bulk of the activity and motivation must come from the employee. Unfortunately, in the vast majority of so-called appraisal and development interviews that are conducted, the bulk of the activity and motivation comes from *the supervisor*. Is it any wonder that the amount of behavior change that has taken place as a result of these interviews has been small indeed?

Realistically, we recognize that many employees are not yet ready for complete responsibility. Some of them require more help from the supervisor, at least initially. It may be that the actual line of progress through the process will be more down the middle of the diagram. However, it should be recognized that the farther to the right of the diagram the activity can be moved, the greater will be the likelihood of favorable behavior change.

SUMMARY

The supervisor's role in bringing about favorable behavior change in an employee is strictly supportive. The employee is the only one who can actually change her or his own behavior. However, through a systematic approach and with a real effort to understand the employee's point of view, the supervisor can play a major role in bringing the employee to the place where he or she can and will change behavior patterns for the benefit of all concerned.

9

The Development Interview

As was pointed out earlier, all the supervisor's analysis and planning, no matter how much that may be, will not by itself bring about any improvement in the employee or in their interpersonal relations. Any attempt to use these efforts to establish a plan for improvement can only be implemented through some communication between the supervisor and the employee. Under most circumstances, the most effective form of communication for this purpose is the interview.

We will focus our attention here specifically on the Development Interview, although most of the principles and approaches covered will apply in virtually any interview situation. Since there are many fine writings on employee counseling and interviewing (see the Bibliography for suggestions), and since our prime purpose in this book is not an examination of interviewing techniques, our treatment of the subject here will merely highlight some of the key considerations related to the Development Interview. Also, it will deal more specifically with the *formal* interview that is held on a regularly scheduled basis rather than the informal spontaneous ones that are probably conducted much more frequently.

PREPARATION STEPS

Perhaps it goes without saying, but the success of any development interview will depend to a large extent on the degree of preparation that both the supervisor and the employee go through prior to the actual interview. Chapters 4 through 7 deal with many of the specifics related to the subject matter for discussion.

It is important to remember that an interview is a structured or planned interpersonal situation. It is an INTER-VIEW, not a casual conversation. It should enable each of the participants to get an insight into the point of view of the other person with a desired outcome being a common viewpoint that is acceptable to both parties. A specific time should be set aside for it in a place where uninterrupted privacy is assured. In addition, there must be a clear understanding on the part of both participants as to the purpose of the interview. Furthermore, some specific objectives for the interview itself need to be established. These may be related to improving job performance, clarifying responsibilities, increasing chances for growth and promotion, assessing priorities, or similar subject areas. Only when you have a clear picture of what goals are realistic and achievable can you go about the process of planning how you will conduct the actual interview. Recognize also that these objectives need not necessarily be accomplished all at one time. The interview may have to be conducted in several stages. It may be that identification of the problem will be all that can be accomplished in one sitting and that any discussion of possible solutions will have to wait for subsequent sessions.

An inherent part of the methodology used in the interview will depend on the personality and general motivation of the employee. Therefore, a careful analysis should be made of the employee's background and on-the-job history. The supervisor should consider this in addition to personal analysis of the employee in order to determine what approach will be most productive.

The Development Interview Checklist, which is included at the end of this chapter, provides an easy-to-follow list of points to be covered prior to, during, and following the actual interview.

CONDUCTING THE INTERVIEW

Assuming that you are approaching the interview in line with the concepts discussed earlier in this book, there are two basic elements that need to be covered: (1) the *evaluation of results* of the employee's performance against objectives, standards, and other factors set during the last review; and (2) the *establishment of objectives and plans* for the next period. Everything of substance discussed in the interview should be related to either or both of these elements. Actually, this allows for much more latitude than may appear at first glance, because anything pertaining to job performance *can* be related to one or both of them. The emphasis in the interview, of course, needs to be on *performance* and, more specifically, on performance factors that make a meaningful contribution to a discussion around *evaluating results* or *establishing objectives and plans.* Let's examine each of these elements briefly in reverse order.

Establishing objectives and plans, as we have pointed out several times, is really the most critical part of the appraisal and development process. Herein lies the whole concept of *joint commitment and action,* which is the essence of any effective effort in this direction. It is particularly important since it comes to grips with the question of achieving compatibility between the individual's and the organization's goals. Here the supervisor can play a significant role in assisting the employee in clarifying personal goals and establishing the relationship of those goals with the goals of the organization. This may well call on all the interviewing skills and counseling techniques the supervisor may have. However, with the achievement of a true commitment to specific goals on the part of the employee, the appraisal and development process is largely self-administering.

Evaluating results, of course, is a joint examination of how the employee's performance measures up against the objectives and plans established during the last review or as modified in the interim. If the objective-setting process was handled properly the last time out and there has been any kind of realistic communication between the two since that time, the evaluation discussion should hold no significant surprises for either party. It should serve primarily to clarify key issues, analyze jointly what went well and where improvements could be made, and place the employee's *total* performance into the proper perspective so that realistic objectives can be set for the next period.

Counseling Techniques*

Here we are not talking about psychological counseling as such, but rather as a communication process whereby the supervisor can assist an employee in dealing with job-related problems in a nonthreatening atmosphere. Let it be perfectly clear, however, that we are in no way attempting to turn the average supervisor into an amateur psychiatrist. Even if the potential hazards in having the supervisor counsel an employee on personal problems were not so obvious, the supervisor rarely has either the time or the training to perform such a service.

The supervisor's concern in the counseling process is to find ways of helping an employee develop or accept an idea or a plan that will lead to mutual on-the-job benefit. We accept an idea or a plan when we believe in it or when, from our point of view, it makes sense.

From the typist's point of view, the supervisor is being downright "picayunish" to have that memo retyped because of a minor error. While the supervisor may agree, there may also be an awareness that the department head is bound to make a remark about the error. Moreover, he or she may also believe that overall impressions are built on just such minor incidents. Now, if the supervisor and the typist and the department head all shared the same point of view, there would be no problem.

In a job performance interview, the important thing to accomplish is an examination of viewpoints. The other person's viewpoint may act as a barrier to the understanding of your problem or vice versa. If both the employee and

*Portions of this section are adapted and excerpted from the Discussion Leader's Guide to *The Engineering of Agreement,* Roundtable Films, Beverly Hills, California.

the supervisor could see a problem the same way, chances are they would both come up with a similar solution.

Viewpoints are not always anchored in cement. They do change. Sometimes they change during conversation. Examples:

"You know—I never thought of it that way before."

"You may have a point there."

"Say that again. I'm not sure I understood you."

"That's a novel way of looking at it."

One effective method of helping others examine their point of view is to get them talking about it. We ordinarily examine our thoughts before we put them into words. Moreover, if we put them into the wrong words, we hasten to correct. ("That isn't what I meant," or "I think I'm trying to say that. . . .")

In order to get this process started, the supervisor has to listen, which is not easy. One way to get in the listening habit is to ask questions. When we use questions to direct the other's attention, we accomplish three things:

1. We commit ourselves to listen to the answer.

2. We help to develop the other person's point of view on the subject.

3. We gain an opportunity to test our own point of view in light of the other person's reasoning.

Here are three types of questions (as illustrated in Roundtable Productions's excellent film *The Engineering of Agreement*) that you may find helpful in resolving differing points of view. They will help both you and your employee to get a better understanding of each other's problems.

Open Questions.   These type questions are ones that cannot be answered yes or no; questions that invite a true expression of opinion and feelings regardless of whether or not they are favorable to your point of view. For example:

"How do you feel about . . . ?"

"What do you think of . . . ?"

The advantages of using *open questions* are:

1. They show your interest in the other person. We are all flattered when others are interested in us and what we think.

2. They make the other person more comfortable and secure because they put her or him "in the driver's seat."

3. They get the other person to think about your plan.

4. They draw the other person out, letting you learn more about the individual and what's on his or her mind. The answers tell you where the real blocks are so that you can design your approach accordingly.

5. They "protect" the other person from making a firm yes or no commitment (which there may be a feeling of obligation to defend) until there has been an opportunity to examine all aspects of the plan.

Reflection.   This is the repetition or rephrasing in your own words of what the other person is trying to say or seems to feel. The first essential factor in reflection is careful listening, and the second is selectivity. To properly reflect the other person's feeling, you must really listen and not be thinking about your own plan or what you are going to say next. Then you have to select the most important idea or feeling from what that person has said, and put it into your own words. Reflection does several things:

1. It is a good way of avoiding argument because it enables you to respond without either rejecting or accepting what has been said.

2. It shows that you understand what was said. If your reflection is in error, the other person can correct you. This, in itself, can go a long way toward creating mutual understanding.

3. The sharing of feelings tends to create a climate for agreement.

4. If the other person has been illogical or irrational (basing ideas on false fears), she or he will very often be able to see the error better when it is expressed nonjudgmentally by you.

5. If the idea expressed is a bad one, it may be dropped or forgotten once you indicate that you understand it.

6. Reflection enables the other person to pick up the main idea in order to continue a logical progression.

7. It encourages further expression or clarification.

Directive Questions.   These questions request expansion or further explanation on one particular point. Generally speaking, you should hold these directive questions off until you have had a complete expression of feelings and opinions so that you understand the other person's point of view as much as possible. Directive questions keep two-way communications going, but also accomplish some things in which you are directly interested. For example:

"Since you agree that . . . , how can we . . . ?"

"You said that you liked . . . , then what can we do to make . . . more acceptable?"

Directive questions have these advantages:

1. They give you more information about the employee's thinking on points where you need such information.

2. They tend to make the employee more favorable toward your position because the more exploration there is in the area of agreement, the less important the area of disagreement will seem.

3. They give the employee the opportunity to be personally convinced. When there is a chance to concentrate on the positive factors, very often the employee will realize the advantages to accepting your plan.

There is an inherent danger in the use of directive questions. It is the temptation that exists, conscious or not, for the supervisor or interviewer to use this approach in a manipulative way—in effect, to use an employee's words to prove a point that may not take into consideration the employee's own needs and concerns. This may result in the short-term accomplishment of some specific objectives the supervisor has in mind. However, it will almost invariably backfire in the long run once it becomes apparent to the employee (as it will) that she or he has been "had."

The real impact of directive questions as a positive communications tool depends on the degree of openness and trust that exists between the supervisor and the employee. How do you build the kind of openness and trust necessary for this impact? Obviously not through a few well-selected questions in a single interview situation. This must be built up over a period of time and must be reinforced by subsequent action on the part of both individuals. If this openness and trust does exist, and if there is a real desire to achieve better understanding and a mutually beneficial agreement, then directive questions are an extremely valuable tool.

These three types of questions will not be the magic formula that will make every interview successful, nor do we recommend their exclusive use in any interview. We do suggest that they can be a tremendously effective means of drawing the other party into a meaningful discussion so that you both can examine the situation from as near a common base of understanding as possible.

Interviewing Hints

In addition to the effective use of *questions* and the corresponding attention to *listening* described earlier, there are some other particularly useful techniques and hints that will make most interviews more meaningful and productive. (The use of the word *technique* here is intended in its best interpretation—as a useful tool for improving the communication process, not as a manipulative device.)

The *You-We* technique is one of the very few methods with which we can virtually guarantee improved communication between a supervisor and employee if it is not already being used. Simply stated, we use "You" to compliment, and "We" to criticize. ("*You* are doing a great job." "*We* have a problem.") The intent here is to make the compliment a *personal* thing and the criticism an *impersonal* thing. It is amazing how much easier it is for me to talk about a problem that *we* have than it is to talk about a problem that *I* have. This makes the issue one of solving the problem rather than one of fixing the blame. Also, realistically, isn't it true that if one of your employees has a problem, you have one, too?

The *second-hand compliment* is one that the supervisor receives from a third party about the performance of an employee. To have a supervisor say, "It made me feel good to hear Mr. Smith say what a great job you did for him" is probably worth twenty comments of direct praise from the supervisor, if given and received sincerely. Yet, think about how often we receive comments from others that could be passed on and we never quite get around to it! What a golden opportunity to build a stronger relationship with an employee! Take advantage of every such opportunity that you can.

The *advice-request* is one of the sincerest forms of flattery you can use—providing you are truly sincere. Asking an employee's advice on something or asking how to handle a particular job that he or she does well suggests that the employee knows more than you do. This technique will frequently get someone to open up who might not do so otherwise.

The *turnabout* is useful when an employee has difficulty in recognizing the negative impact she or he may be having on others. In this approach, the supervisor gets the employee to analyze his or her own feelings in a certain situation and then draws a parallel to that employee's own behavior. For example, an employee who gets upset when a typist refuses to do some work may be brought to realize that it was the employee's approach to that typist that created the very attitude that is so irritating.

The *summary* ought to be a part of every interview, but more often than not it is overlooked. Actually, it can be one of the most useful tools the supervisor can use. Have you ever conducted an interview that went on too long, with the result that any progress that had been made earlier was lost? Wouldn't you have liked to have been able to close it off at the peak? You probably could have with a *summary*. When you sense that you have reached that point in an interview where you have accomplished all you can reasonably hope to in that sitting, introduce a *summary* with a phrase like one of these, using words that are comfortable to you:

"Well, let's review some of the things we have discussed today. . . ."

"Here's my understanding of the points we've touched on. . . ."

"Looking back over our discussion. . . ."

The use of a *summary* in this manner accomplishes three specific things: (1) It makes it quite clear the interview is coming to an end. (2) If the discussion has wandered off course a bit (which is quite common), you can bring it back on target by reiterating the key points you want carried away from the interview. (3) Responsibility can be established for key actions that should come as a result of the discussion. With a little practice, the *summary* is not a difficult tool to use, and it is an invaluable one in any interview situation, regardless of which side of the table you are on.

Finally, we cannot emphasize enough the importance of *sincerity* as an essential element in the interview process. By this we do not mean to adopt the attitude of the cynic who says, "Always be sincere whether you mean it or not." A lack of a sincere desire on the part of the supervisor to achieve a better working relationship will shine through like a beacon. *You are better off not conducting the interview at all if you cannot approach it with a sincere interest in the other person's point of view.*

EVALUATING THE INTERVIEW

There has never yet been an interview that went perfectly. This should not be disturbing, however, provided the interviewer learns from the mistakes that have been made. A participant in a training program on interviewing made the following comment at the class session following one in which he had done some role playing: "All the way home after our last class, I practiced my 'shudaseds'." He had coined a particularly graphic word to describe part of the evaluation process. The supervisor should carefully review everything that took place in an interview, including what should have been said and what should not have been said. Obviously, what has already happened cannot be undone, but it should serve as a positive base from which to more effectively conduct the next interview.

The Development Interview Checklist is a good tool to use as a basis for evaluating an interview. It points out the steps to be followed and some of the pitfalls to avoid. For maximum benefit, it is important that the supervisor review and evaluate the way the interview was conducted as soon as possible after it is completed, making notes for use in improving future interviews.

FOLLOW-UP RESPONSIBILITIES

Much of what would be normal follow-up activity has already been discussed. In addition, however, it is essential that a written record be made of the interview for three principal reasons.

1. To provide a written agreement and understanding reached between the supervisor and the employee as to the commitments made by each and the plan of action to accomplish them (each should retain a copy)

2. To maintain a continuing record of the employee's progress and development and to serve as a memory recall tool for the supervisor

3. To serve as a review device for future action when appropriate

If the organization has a formal performance appraisal form, it may be sufficient to meet this requirement; however, for future assistance, the supervisor may want more information than such a form can provide. In that case, the worksheets found in Chapter 6 or a Memo-to-File with a narrative report of the significant points covered may be helpful.

One other point that relates to follow-up is the matter of frequency of interviewing. This will vary widely with each individual employee's requirements. We recommend that a formal development interview be held at least once each year, and a progress review at least once a quarter with every employee. Progress reviews are interim discussions between formal review periods where the supervisor and the employee have an opportunity to review progress to date on those objectives and plans agreed to earlier. It includes reviewing what is going well, what is not going well and what corrective actions are or need to be taken, and what is different now from what existed at the time of the original agreement. If the circumstances are sufficiently different (anticipated resources, human and otherwise, do not become available; new priorities have been established; a radical change has developed that causes original plans to be obsolete; etc.), then the appraisal and development plan should be modified to reflect reality. Without this flexibility, the appraisal and development process can become a meaningless exercise.

For some employees (the top performers, the self-starters, the steady workers), a yearly formal review with quarterly progress reviews may be sufficient—a mere summarizing of informal discussions held on an ongoing basis. For many others, a formal review every three to six months, with monthly progress reviews, seems especially productive. For still others, an even greater frequency may be desirable. A new employee, for example, may need formal monthly, or even weekly, reviews during the early stages. The supervisor must analyze each employee and make the determination in each case as to how often such an interview can be of mutual benefit. While this may seem like a heavy investment of time for a supervisor, it well may represent the single most important job that the supervisor has—helping to improve the performance of his or her employees.

SUMMARY

The Development Interview is one of the most critical and useful tools that a supervisor has for effectively increasing the efficiency of operations and taking maximum advantage of all available resources. In addition, it is truly one of the most valuable instruments for assisting the affected employee in working toward full potential. This chapter has barely scratched the surface in the techniques of effective interviewing. We strongly recommend further study and practice for those wishing to expand their capabilities in this area.

Development Interview Checklist

Keep uppermost in your mind that the purpose of the development interview is to review past performance with the employee compared with mutually agreed-upon performance factors and objectives, and to mutually draw up plans for furthering the employee's growth and development.

I. Preparation for the Interview

A. Make sure you know what was mutually understood in terms of job duties, standards, performance factors, objectives, assignments, and any other predetermined criteria for evaluation.

B. Review employee's background.
   1. Education
   2. Training
   3. Experience

C. Review the employee's past jobs and job performance.

D. Observe job performance measured against job expectations.
   1. Make sure sufficient observations are made.
   2. Avoid pitfalls:
      —Bias
      —Memory
      —Failure to observe all job duties
      —Concentrating on jobs in trouble
      —Allowing your experience to prejudice judgment
      —Observing handiest jobs only

E. Determine the strengths and development needs to be discussed with the employee.
   1. Be certain to have specific, unbiased observations that can be used in connection with each.
   2. Don't try to make too many critical points. Decide in advance which areas have a practical chance of being improved and prepare to discuss only these unless others are raised by the employee.

F. For each need you intend to discuss with the employee, be prepared with a possible development plan to propose should he or she need assistance in coming up with a suitable plan.

G. Determine those points you do *not* intend to discuss with the employee and how you plan to handle them.

H. Identify areas for concentration during the next review period.

I. Make certain the employee is aware of the planned discussion in sufficient time to do his or her own preparation.

II. Conducting the Interview
  A. Beginning the discussion:
      1. Set the stage.
         —Informality and a friendly atmosphere are important
         —Be sincere—be yourself
      2. Explain the purpose of the discussion.
      3. Make it clear that the discussion is a two-way conversation—a mutual problem-solving and goal-setting exchange.
  B. Body of the discussion:
      1. Talk job performance—employee strengths and improvement needs— evaluating results of performance against objectives set during last review.
      2. Talk about strong points first, alternating, interspersing, and blending the discussion of improvement needs with discussion of strong points.
      3. Be prepared to cite observations you have made for each point you wish to discuss.
      4. Encourage the employee to appraise his or her own performance.
         —Use OPEN and DIRECTIVE questions
         —Use REFLECTION and restatement of the employee's remarks to provide opportunity for self-examination of their logic and to help the employee reach an understanding of related problems
      5. Before discussing the suggestions you may have, let the employee tell you what development plans he or she may have.
         —Try to get the employee to set personal targets
         —Your mission is to *help* in their achievement
      6. Reach agreement on development plans with the employee. Plans should spell out what you are going to do and what the employee intends to do.
      7. Establish work objectives jointly for the next period.
  C. Ending the discussion:
      1. Summarize what has been discussed.
         —Make it positive
         —Show enthusiasm for the plans you and the employee have made
      2. Give the employee an opportunity to make any additional suggestions.
      3. Close discussion on a friendly, harmonious note.

III. Post-Interview Activity
  A. Make a record of:
      1. Plans you and employee have made (with a copy to the employee).
      2. Points requiring follow-up.
      3. Commitments you have made for action on your part.
  B. Evaluate how you handled the discussion.
      1. What did you do well?
      2. What did you do poorly? How would you do it differently?
      3. What did you learn about the employee? About your job?
  C. Resolve to do an even better job next time!

10

"The Scorecard"—
Documentation, Forms, and
Compensation

Our position that the performance appraisal process has, as its primary value, the improvement of performance and the development of people has been made abundantly clear in this book thus far. Properly utilized, we see it as one of the most effective supervisory tools available and one that can have tremendous impact on an organization. However, we would be naive if we believed that most supervisors are ready, willing, and able to invest the time and energy necessary to make a performance appraisal system work for those reasons alone. There are some far more urgent (albeit less important) reasons that tend to force supervisory action in this regard. These are largely related to the requirement made by most organizations for a supervisor to complete that annual "scorecard" for each direct report. This, of course, is designed to document an employee's performance presumably to improve and support managerial decisions related to compensation, promotions, reassignments, and adverse actions. This leads to a need that supervisors have for proper documentation—the third supervisory skill area identified in Chapter 1.

NEED FOR DOCUMENTATION

More than ever before in our history, accurate and specific information on individual employee performance is absolutely essential. There was a time when an employee's personnel records could be held strictly confidential, even from the affected employee. The law now requires that all such records must be made available to that employee on request. In many cases, this places the supervisor in a "damned if you do and damned if you don't" situation. On the one hand, an employee could challenge any statements the supervisor might make, forcing a defense of such statements. Even an extremely complimentary review could backfire if the employee does not receive an anticipated increase or promotion. The possibility of such challenges has caused many supervisors to take the path of least resistance, using relatively safe, meaningless statements implying a level of performance that is satisfactory or better. On the other hand, if certain personnel actions are taken and there is not a documented record that clearly supports such actions, there is an excellent chance that both the organization *and the supervisor* may, at one extreme, be very embarrassed or, at the other extreme, be liable for civil or criminal action.

The Appendix contains an interesting and revealing article by Morris Bryson, entitled "Documentation—Its Importance in Performance Appraisal." He makes an extremely strong case related to the legal and ethical implications of proper documentation, together with some specific recommendations for management action. Without duplicating the ideas presented in that article, we will identify briefly some of the needs for and uses of proper documentation.

1. **Legal recourse.**   The Bryson article addresses this issue in detail. We have barely seen the "tip of the iceberg" on the legal consequences of improper or inadequate documentation.

2. **Evidence of equity in treatment.**   Aside from the potential legal requirements, proper documentation will increase the probability of consistent application of personnel policies and practices throughout an organization. Through some sort of audit procedure, formal or informal, it is possible to determine the extent to which personnel decisions are equitable and, where necessary, to bring about appropriate changes in personnel practices.

3. **Support for personnel decisions.**   When a tentative personnel decision has been made that will require approval by others, a supervisor is in a much stronger position to get positive action in the approval cycle with accurate, specific, and consistent documentation that backs up that decision. This relates to positive decisions—salary increases, incentive pay, promotions, special awards, etc.—as well as negative decisions—disciplinary action, no salary increases, downgrades, terminations, etc.

4. **Mutual clarification of expectations.**   Since we have placed heavy emphasis on the use of performance appraisal as a projection of expected performance, as well as an evaluation of past performance, the documentation of mutually understood performance expectations provides both the employee and the supervisor with a tool they can use to work toward improved performance. The ability of either to refer back to this documentation substantially reduces the likelihood of surprises or misunderstandings when evaluation time comes along.

5. **Reminders at review time.**   Since very few people have total recall, documentation of the original understanding, any modifications to that understanding, plus specific actions related to that understanding that are documented as they occur, provides both the supervisor and the employee with a point of reference during progress reviews as well as at performance evaluation time.

6. Reinforcement of mutually understood action. Aside from the value at review time, documentation serves as a tangible reminder to both parties that there is a need to carry out certain specified actions. It increases the likelihood that such action will take place.

PERFORMANCE APPRAISAL FORMS

You will notice that there are no examples of either "good" or "poor" appraisal forms in this book. There are two reasons for this. First, we have not seen, nor have we been able to create, a form with which we would be totally comfortable under all organizational circumstances. Consequently, publishing one or even several recommended forms is an open invitation to nitpicking, particularly when it is the process and not the form that is the key to effective performance appraisals. Second, and perhaps more important, is the fact that the vast majority of supervisors who will be reading this book will have little, if any, influence on how such a form is created. Holding certain appraisal forms up as better than others may cause added dissatisfaction with the form that is currently in use in the organization, which could be counterproductive to what we are trying to accomplish here.

While we are not recommending a specific form, there are some elements we would like to see incorporated into an appraisal form because we feel they will improve the usefulness of that form. The specific way they are addressed, whether on the form itself or as an adjunct to it, should be within the province of those in the organization charged with that responsibility.

Space for Entering Performance Expectations. This should provide the opportunity for the employee and the supervisor to jointly agree on the major accomplishments to be achieved during the projected measurement period. It should permit the inclusion of any variations on the appraisal models introduced in this book, either on the form itself or as an adjunct to it.

Space for Entering Modifications. When circumstances justify, there should be an opportunity for modifying portions of the agreement to reflect additional requirements or significant changes in priorities. Again, this could be an adjunct to the form itself but, without some flexibility in the process to accommodate legitimate changing circumstances, its value will be substantially reduced if not lost entirely. At the very least, there needs to be provision for an explanation when results achieved (for valid reasons) are different from what was projected. This does not mean that projections should be changed just because we are not going to make them, but because such a change is in the best interests of both the organization and the employee.

Space for Recording Accomplishments. What was or was not accomplished toward the expectations established needs to be recorded somewhere on the form. In addition, there should be an opportunity to record other significant accomplishments or nonaccomplishments that reflect on the overall performance of the individual, even though they may not have been included in the expectations, provided that the nonaccomplishments do not come as a surprise to the employee.

Space for Recording Performance Strengths and Areas for Improvement. Note that we are referring to *performance* strengths, not traits or characteristics. Descriptions should be results oriented (e.g., "others seek and receive employee's assistance on team projects" rather than "cooperative"). Also note that we are addressing areas for improvement, not weaknesses (e.g., "needs to increase percent of on-time deliveries" rather than "always late"). We avoid the word *weakness* because an employee who may be performing satisfactorily still has room for improvement if the result of that improvement justifies the effort required. Identified areas for improvement should be backed up with objectives or action plans for their achievement.

There may be other elements that are worthy of inclusion on a performance appraisal form. The factors listed here are not intended to be all-inclusive. They do cover those areas that place heavy emphasis on what a person *does* rather than what a person *is*.

Adapt, Don't Adopt

Since most supervisors must work within whatever performance appraisal system may be in existence within the organization, we feel it is important that they *adapt* the approach to performance appraisal described in this book so that it can be used within the existing system. If the form that is provided lends itself to the inclusion of one of the models in some manner, then that is the logical way to go. If the prescribed form does not allow that kind of adaptation, then our recommendation is for the supervisor, together with the employee, to develop the model that is most appropriate and work from that as the primary tool for guiding performance. Then, using that model as the prime data source, complete the form in line with organizational instructions. The appraisal model and recorded performance against it then becomes the supervisor's backup in the event further information is needed to support whatever entries are made on the appraisal form.

PERFORMANCE APPRAISALS AND COMPENSATION

Inevitably, there comes the time when a supervisor must either make or recommend a decision related to an employee's compensation. Whether this is referred to as pay for performance, merit pay, incentive pay, bonus, annual increase, or whatever, some adjustment in an employee's compensation normally is expected. This kind of decision making is a mixed blessing for most supervisors. If there is an unlimited merit budget and all employees are truly outstanding, this is not a problem. (Do you know any situations where both those conditions exist?) In the early 1970s (well before CSRA), the U.S. Postal Service removed all salaried employees above a certain grade level from automatic progression (regular step increases) and placed them in a merit plan whereby their salaries were adjusted annually by management decisions based on performance. There was loud cheering from most middle- and upper-level managers that "we can finally reward people for performance rather than longevity." This "cheering" continued until the first review date when the overwhelming majority of increases were given "across the board," with very few significant differences based on individual performance.

Making differential compensation decisions is difficult for most supervisors, because in order for some employees to receive higher than average increases, some other employees must receive either lower than average increases or no increases at all. Consequently, the automatic granting of step increases, based on length of service, makes supervisory decision making a lot easier. As a result, many supervisors who operate under some form of merit review still prefer to grant equal increases to virtually all of their employees.

Assuming that compensation decisions will be made on some basis that incorporates more than length of service, there are four important factors that must influence these decisions: employee performance, the organization's financial condition, internal pay relationships, and external pay relationships.

Employee performance obviously should have a significant effect on compensation decisions affecting that employee. Clearly, for any kind of a merit system to work, high performers must be rewarded commensurate with their contributions or there is a good chance they will be looking for employment elsewhere. The key to that, of course, is in coming up with meaningful criteria by which the term *high performer* can be defined. The discussion of criteria earlier in this book should help in that definition. One word of caution—avoid like the plague placing yourself in a position of committing to specified increases for specified levels of performance. First of all, you may not be able to deliver on that commitment because of circumstances beyond your control. Second, such an approach is an open invitation to "games playing," whereby either the expectations or the recorded results may be "adjusted" to paint an unrealistically favorable picture.

The organization's financial condition has to be a major consideration when it comes to making compensation decisions. Whether an organization's budget is determined on the basis of anticipated sales or revenue, growth projections, corporate allocation, or divine guidance, there will be times when the amount of money available for distribution as increased compensation will be considerably less than at other times. This means that even a truly outstanding employee may receive a lower increase during a lean period than what an average performer might get during more affluent times.

Internal pay relationships addresses the issue of parity of pay among people in similar positions. For most salaried employees, compensation is far more of a status issue than it is an economic issue. Since relatively few are facing economic survival, the compensation one employee receives is viewed more as a symbol of personal worth when compared with others, individually or collectively. Furthermore, if you are laboring under the delusion that pay records can and will be held confidential, you are naive, to say the least. Anyone who wants to find out what someone else is making will find it out one way or another. Therefore, you are much safer in assuming that everyone in your group knows the compensation being received by everyone else, regardless of whether or not it is a published record. Since, as most behaviorists agree, fair pay does not motivate but unfair pay demotivates, you cannot afford to have too great a disparity in compensation received by people in similar positions. Consequently, employees who perform satisfactorily (but not outstandingly) still must be recognized in the paycheck even if it means there will be less to distribute to the superior performers. Otherwise, the "satisfactory" employees are likely to become dissatisfied, which could lead to considerably less than satisfactory performance.

External pay relationships refers to an employee's perceived value in the market place. The law of supply and demand frequently dictates the pay an employee with certain skills will receive. Regardless of contribution to the organization, there is a strong likelihood that an employee with skills that are readily available in the labor market will receive less of an increase than one whose skills are in short supply. While this may appear unfair, it is a fact of life. Since part of the reason for providing additional compensation is the retention of valued employees, their ability to command a higher rate of pay elsewhere will influence compensation decisions affecting them.

There are no easy answers to dealing with these and other factors when it comes time to make or recommend compensation decisions. We feel it is more productive to address these factors head on and determine ahead of time, individually or in consultation with other managers in your organization, what part each of these factors will play in those decisions, and, more importantly, how you will interpret them to your employees.

There are several techniques for arriving at specific compensation decisions for individuals or groups of individuals. These include such approaches as *individual salary curves, peer ranking, survey data,* and a *marketability formula.* Since most supervisors in business and industry have relatively little to say about the approach to be followed, we will not attempt to describe them here. If you are interested in exploring these further, see any of the books on compensation listed in our Bibliography or, better still, consult a compensation specialist who can advise you which approach, or combination of approaches, makes the most sense for you.

SUMMARY

In spite of our insistence that performance appraisal should be used primarily for the improvement of performance and the development of people, we cannot ignore the fact that completing the annual "scorecard" is one of the first things supervisors think of when the subject comes up. This inevitably raises the issues of *documentation,* use of *forms,* and *compensation.*

Documentation, particularly its legal and ethical implications, is addressed specifically in the Appendix, "Documentation—Its Importance in Performance Appraisal" by Morris Bryson. Proper documentation is now an essential supervisory skill as a safeguard against legal recourse, evidence of equity in treatment, support for personnel decisions, mutual clarification of expectations, reminders at review time, and reinforcement of mutually understood action.

We have deliberately avoided publishing examples of "good" or "poor" appraisal *forms.* We believe very strongly that it is the process, not the form, that makes for effective performance appraisals. Furthermore, most supervisors must work with whatever forms are in use in their organizations anyway. The appraisal models described earlier in this book can be adapted for use with virtually any appraisal forms currently in use in public sector organizations. A supervisor needs to address the following four elements either on the form itself or as a part of his or her backup documentation: space for entering performance expectations, space for entering modifications based on changing circumstances, space for recording accomplishments, and space for recording performance strengths and areas for improvement.

Compensation decisions, whether made directly or recommended by the supervisor, are a mixed blessing. Since, in most corporate organizations today, length of service is no longer the prime consideration at review time, differential decisions based on employee performance are a requirement. The criteria developed as a result of recommendations made earlier in this book will help in those decisions. However, as important as individual employee performance may be, it is not the sole determinant when it comes to making those decisions. Other factors that will influence those decisions include the organization's financial condition, internal pay relationships, and external pay relationships. Careful thought must be given to each of these prior to the time the decisions are made and then interpreted to the affected employees.

The "scorecard" is there. We cannot avoid it. Let's make sure it works for us, not against us.

11

Summary—Making It Work for You

The performance appraisal is one of the most misunderstood and least effectively used tools available to the manager. Both the advent of employment-related legislation and the heavy attention that has been given to the legal consequences of improperly documenting the performance of employees have presented a somewhat distorted view as to the value of this tool. So much emphasis has been placed on the *negative* impact of *not doing* an effective job of performance appraisal that the *positive* benefits of *doing* an effective job have not received the attention they deserve. While we have addressed both the legal and the negative aspects of performance appraisals in this book, we have placed much heavier emphasis on the many positive values to be achieved from proper use. Performance appraisals can be *the key to effective supervision.*

Effective use of the performance appraisal process is dependent on three distinct sets of supervisory skills which *can be learned.* These skills are related to establishing *performance measurement criteria, interpersonal communications* (before, during, and after the performance measurement period), and *documentation.* By helping supervisors develop their skills in these three areas, there are many benefits, both loss avoided and value added, that can accrue to the organization, the supervisor, and the individual employee (supervisee), as addressed in Chapter 1.

In order for the performance appraisal process to be truly effective, several departures from tradition are essential: (1) achieving an appropriate balance between *objective and subjective measures,* concentrating on what an employee *does* rather than what an employee *is;* (2) using a *tailored rather than a standard approach,* adapting to both the position and the incumbent; (3) *separating performance appraisal from the multipurpose evaluation,* focusing on performance improvement at a time that is apart from decisions related to salary, promotion, disciplinary action, etc.; and (4) emphasizing the importance of *joint action and commitment* between the supervisor and the employee. The focus is far more on the *future* than on the past and, properly administered, the appraisal and development process can be largely *self-administering.*

The performance appraisal process raises all sorts of additional issues that tend to complicate the supervisor's role in making the process work. These include such things as the conflict that exists in some organizations over what role the Personnel, Industrial Relations, or Human Resources Department should play in making the process work, the relation to unions, documentation requirements, and additional complications when working in a matrix organization or with direction from a parent company. We have addressed each of these issues specifically in Chapter 2 with some suggestions of ways to reduce the frustrations that are bound to arise. We also called particular attention to the impact of the post-World War II "baby boom" crunch and how the performance appraisal process can be used to ease some of the problems likely to come up as a result. Properly administered, performance appraisals should be seen as a supervisory help, not a hindrance.

Working from both the philosophy and approach of *Management by Objectives and Results* (MOR), we have identified three appraisal and development models that can be tailored to specific positions and individuals. These are: (1) a *three-sectioned approach* that incorporates *key results areas* (critical elements, functional requirements, major responsibilities, etc.), *work objectives and assignments,* and *personal development objectives;* (2) the *MOR Agreement* (for those following that approach to management); and (3) an approach for jobs that have similar and repetitive factors in which we identify *tasks/responsibilities* and *performance standards* for those repetitive factors, followed up with *problem-solving* and *innovative objectives.*

The same three models were applied to managerial positions with particular emphasis on the four general areas in which a manager/supervisor should be evaluated: *unit output, self output, performance in the functions of management,* and *performance and development of employees.* We also addressed the use of objectives and results in managerial career planning. From the perspective of both the organization and the individual manager, the importance of bringing about a joint understanding of appropriate career goals and determining the most effective way of achieving them requires an objectives-oriented approach to performance appraisal.

Performance standards have become the most talked about step in many performance appraisal systems. Attention to them frequently tends to evoke emotions ranging from fear and trepidation at one extreme to apathy or derision at the other. Yet the establishment of specific expectations, whether we call them standards, objectives, or something else, is absolutely essential to any kind of a planned approach to appraisal and development. We have identified six primary steps to such an approach with performance standards at the heart:

1. Know what you expect.
   a. Tasks/responsibilities, key results areas, or critical elements
   b. Performance standards, objectives, or assignments

2. Observe job performance.

3. Compare performance expectations with results.

4. Develop plan to improve performance results.

5. Use progress or development interview to motivate employee.

6. Carry out development plans and evaluate results.

To be meaningful, standards must be *realistic and achievable,* should be set *slightly above average,* and should be *subject to change* as needed. Three types of evaluation are used to establish standards: (1) *predetermined standards,* (2) comparison with the *performance of others,* and (3) comparison with the *employee's own performance.*

Failure of an employee to meet a standard could be caused by any or all of three different contributing factors: (1) *the employee's performance,* (2) *the supervisor's performance,* and (3) *the situation or job itself.* Each must be examined before jumping to what might be the most obvious (but not necessarily the most appropriate) conclusion. For an employee to satisfactorily meet a performance standard, three conditions must exist. The employee must clearly *understand* what is expected, be *capable* of performing the work, and be *willing* to do it. All three must be present or there is little likelihood of success.

Implicit in the concept of appraisal and development is a desire to bring about some sort of favorable behavior change in the employee. This means, first of all, that we must recognize the difference between behavior change and compliance. Compliance is relatively easy to secure and may be interpreted as behavior change. However, unless the employee feels a real sense of ownership of the projected action, compliance is the best we are likely to get. The key here is in understanding the roles of the supervisor and the employee in the process. If the process is to be effective, the supervisor must play a *supportive* role only. The employee is the only one who can actually change behavior. The supervisor can be an effective facilitator in this process, provided the steps followed are designed to place the responsibility for final determination of action on the shoulders of the employee.

The Development Interview, as conducted following the concepts covered in this book, has two basic elements: (1) *evaluating results* of the employee's performance against objectives or standards set during the last review, and (2) *establishing objectives* for the next period. Establishing objectives is the more critical of the two because it is basic to the whole concept of *joint commitment and action.* If that is done properly, the evaluation aspect becomes more a process of clarification and analysis than one of making a value judgment. The Development Interview Checklist (see page 118) is a useful aid to the supervisor in preparing for, conducting, and later evaluating Development Interview efforts.

Finally, the need for documentation is perhaps the clincher that emphasizes the importance of effective performance appraisals. The criticality of proper performance records for compensation, promotions, and other important decisions, as well as protection against possible legal recourse, has never been more evident. While it is unfortunate that it takes a concern about negative consequences to get our attention, nevertheless the requirement for proper documentation may be the one factor that will force many organizations and many supervisors to give performance appraisals the attention they deserve.

Performance appraisal can be another meaningless paperwork exercise or it can be one of the most useful supervisory tools available. Since there is increasing pressure on managers in all organizations to demonstrate value received and to continually strive for performance improvement, it makes eminently good sense to make positive use of this all-important process. Performance appraisal, properly used, can and should be *the key to effective supervision*. The use of objectives and results in performance appraisals is a logical extension of the management process known as *Management by Objectives and Results*. The key factor in both, of course, is *commitment by people*—and that's really what effective management is all about!

Introduction to
Appendix Article

I am especially pleased about and appreciative of Morris Bryson's efforts in writing the Appendix article on documentation for this book. He has made an in-depth study of the legal ramifications of critical actions and nonactions. In his article, "Documentation—Its Importance in Performance Appraisal," he has clearly spelled out the potential discrimination liability that can face the individual supervisor as well as the organization. He also has some specific recommendations on how to address documentation requirements that will help to avoid or minimize many of the problems associated with improper records.

APPENDIX

Documentation—Its Importance in Performance Appraisal

Morris H. Bryson
Bryson Associates, Inc.
Orinda, California

Under oath, could you testify that every statement you have written in your employee's performance appraisal is true and correct to the best of your knowledge? After all, you are two months late on the scheduled review. Perhaps you feel it will be easier to face your assistant with glowing descriptions—"warm fuzzies"—than to discuss mediocre results. Casually rush through the performance appraisal interview and you may awaken a named defendant along with your employer in a discrimination suit.

All levels of management must take seriously their responsibilities for documentation throughout the process of Management by Objectives and Results (MOR). Documentation is essential to MOR and becoming indispensable as a managerial skill. Managers often deny allegations of discrimination and express deeply hurt feelings because a loyal employee has accused them of it. In courts and the administrative "jungle" of state and federal equal employment regulatory agencies, the single most obvious document that is damaging to defense of discrimination charges is the performance appraisal statement. Denial of promotion is hard to defend when performance appraisal statements describe an employee who "walks on water." The "for cause" discharge of an incompetent employee is indefensible following a glowing performance review and a "merit" wage increase.

Problems of adequate, accurate documentation pervades at all responsibility levels. Hourly paid production workers, professionals, and supervisors are often victims of inaccurately written descriptions of their performance or behavior. Ask any labor attorney who represents the defense in either discrimination cases or arbitration of labor disputes. The labor attorney will confirm that the single most difficult problem in defending management's actions is faulty documentation of performance, behavior, and results.

DISCRIMINATION LIABILITY

Ask a risk manager or insurance manager to research the availability of employment discrimination liability insurance. Your organization, along with its managers and supervisors, needs protection for all levels of management who personally and individually can be sued for acts of employment discrimination. The issues are so complex that insurance companies have not been eager to insure either organizations or managerial personnel against costly damage awards in discrimination suits. One reason why discrimination is not an easily insurable exposure is that it is difficult to defend employment discrimination cases without quality documentation of employee performance to support management's actions.

Discrimination in employment complaints, which are costly (often in the millions of dollars), have in most cases involved classes of employees who alleged to be victims of discriminatory decisions in promotion, job assignments, pay, and discipline. Documentation of each personnel transaction to promote, to assign people to particular jobs, to grant "merit" wage increases, or to discharge from employment generally, is supported or unfortunately not supported, as fair and consistent by performance appraisal papers. Absent from the documents is any evidence of clear standards of expectations or positive, constructive effort to enable a worker to succeed in the job; and frequently there has been no due process in management's handling of the problem employee.

Costly class action awards often involve minorities and women. These classes of protected workers will continue to challenge management. Regulations protecting pregnant workers' job rights, including promotions, will require clear documentation of management decisions. The "reverse discrimination" charges initiated by male Caucasians who allege that they are victims of preferential treatment afforded minorities and women, can be threatening to the organization that does document thoughtful, regular, timely, and candid performance appraisals. Yes, even the white male majority is entitled to equal treatment, including performance appraisals.

Perhaps in the years ahead, even more critical than the challenges from minorities and women, will be documentation to support fair, consistent treatment of employees in four closely related or overlapping categories: (1) age discrimination, (2) handicapped discrimination, (3) alcohol/drug abusers, and (4) victims of wrongful dismissals in violation of express or implied contracts of employment.

AGE DISCRIMINATION AND VOLUNTARY RETIREMENT

With social changes and developments in voluntary retirement regulations, age discrimination will require managerial expertise in MOR. Federal law prohibits compulsory retirement under the age of seventy, and some state laws, such as California's, prohibit compulsory retirement at any age. A sound system for appraisal, plus committed and skilled managers, will be critical to coping with age-related performance issues. The MOR process, especially the documentation and face-to-face communications, will be essential to establishing positive, healthy attitudes toward retirement as a reward rather than management's farewell termination for long-service employees who have "burned out."

Age discrimination and voluntary retirement will challenge management to manage. Inflation and the problems of living on fixed incomes may make voluntary retirement unattractive for workers. No longer can management put long-service employees "on the shelf," with meaningless titles, for the final years before compulsory retirement sweeps them off the payroll with the gold watch. And the courts make it all too clear that older workers cannot be removed to create opportunities for "bright young comers." One landmark age discrimination case went against Standard Oil of California. In the Standard Oil case, over 200 long-service employees were "encouraged" to retire to make room for managerial changes, including promotions of groomed successors who might otherwise leave for greener pastures and promotions in other companies. It is reported that most of the 200 plus individual cases alleging age discrimination were not defensible because performance appraisal documents did not declare failing marks in job performance by the older workers. One personnel executive grumbled that until the age discrimination case, not all divisions of Standard Oil had the management commitment required to assure accurate, documented performance appraisals. Maybe some executives thought of performance appraisal as a Personnel Department program. Standard Oil's settlement was in excess of $2,000,000, plus some reinstatements. Accurate performance appraisals could have prevented that expense, the personal disappointments and hard feelings that were involved, and the adverse publicity.

Individual charges of age discrimination often develop and are lost by management because of inaccurate documentation and ineffective communication. Promotion denial because of age was the charge in one complicated case. A sales management position became open. The thirty-three-year-old "superstar" got the promotion. The complainant, Herb (not his real name), was a fifty-eight-year-old who had been looking forward for many years to the day when he could stop selling and move into management status. Performance appraisal documents indicated that Herb was doing a "good" job. Unfortunately, management failed to tell Herb that his "good" performance was, in fact, less than that of other sales people, and likewise they never told Herb that he produced less sales results than they expected from him. An effective performance appraisal process would have been a valuable tool in management's selection of the sales person deserving promotion, and perhaps Herb would not have been the leading candidate. However, without documentation and frank, accurate communication of performance standards and results, Herb's charge of age discrimination was a costly lesson. In addition to attorney fees, backpay awards, etc., lost management time alone expended in defending this case will exceed the time that would have been required for an effective performance appraisal effort.

DISCRIMINATION AND THE HANDICAPPED WORKER

Federal and state laws that require hiring and advancing handicapped workers parallel the laws protecting women and minorities. Who is handicapped? The definition is broad, including an individual who "has a record of" or "is regarded as having" an impairment. This definition includes the invisibly handicapped such as epileptics, diabetics, and persons who have recovered from mental illness, heart attacks, or cancer. As is true with the aging processes, able-bodied workers after years of service may develop handicap conditions, possibly resulting in diminished capabilities.

Greater management understanding of both visible and invisible handicap conditions will be required. The performance appraisal process need only document the workers' capabilities and achievements, not their disabilities. Crisp, clear, accurate documentation at each step in the MOR process will be important to establishing any required accommodation for specific handicapped workers. If an individual worker's capabilities diminish to the point where performance is unacceptable, or work cannot be performed safely, the justification for transfer or termination must be clearly documented.

ALCOHOL/DRUG ABUSE AND WORKER BEHAVIOR

One shocking problem that perhaps exists in all organizations is the problem drinker or drug user. This very complex problem parallels the age and handicapped discrimination issues just discussed. It is not infrequent that the "problem" worker, protected because the worker is over age forty, is also a problem performer whose employment history is marred by alcohol or drug abuse and whose physical well being is exposed to disabling conditions. Often the individual has a record of outstanding performance, then develops patterns of absenteeism and tell-tale behavior.

Managers need to appreciate that professional experts have enough trouble dealing with all the work-related issues resulting from alcohol and drug abuse. Managers and supervisors need to be responsible and to be responsive to job performance and results, not the analysis of conditions such as alcoholism. Management's job is to provide the opportunity for each worker to perform specific job duties without threat to property or the safety of any person. It is a well established fact that many of the disabling conditions such as alcohol and drug abuse need not result in loss of talented employees if only management will address the symptoms early. The earliest and most obvious symptoms are decreased job performance and increased absenteeism. An effective performance appraisal process administered by skilled, committed managers will detect performance deficiencies, enabling management to restore slipping workers to results-oriented employees; and managers will learn to identify situations where professional help must be sought by the worker. There can be great personal satisfaction for the professional manager who provides the leadership to the troubled worker who slips temporarily but is promptly directed to objectives and results—and that's what it is all about.

WRONGFUL DISCHARGE AND IMPLIED EMPLOYMENT CONTRACTS

Proliferating federal and state prohibitions against discriminatory discharge include race, color, national origin, sex, age, religion, handicapped, and veterans. Collective bargaining agreements provide unionized workers arbitration for challenges to dismissals, and public employees enjoy job security through civil service rules. In addition, the courts are eroding an employer's prerogative to terminate any employee at will. There is an emerging recognition that workers should be free from arbitrary or capricious terminations. This good faith and fair dealing standard carries an implied contract that satisfactory job performance will afford the worker with some degree of job security. Unsatisfactory performance or violation of reasonable rules, following appropriate warnings, can result in "just cause" dismissals.

Employee handbooks, policies and procedures manuals, and established employer's practices generally express or imply fair treatment and career opportunities with permanent employment. Then, if a business takes a downward turn and staff reductions are necessary, or if there is a "blow-up" and someone becomes victim to a heat-of-battle discharge, the combination of implied employment contract and apparent arbitrary dismissal gives rise to charges of "wrongful discharge." Where there has been no formal or written criticism of an employee's performance, or no recorded rule violations, the wrongful discharge victim can turn to the courts. The unjust termination is challenged, alleging breach of express or implied contract, intentional infliction of emotional distress, libel, slander, etc., and asking for punitive damages for pain and suffering.

When is dismissal for "just cause," and when is it a "wrongful discharge"? Those documents on file in the personnel jacket, along with the supervisor's communication skills, will be scrutinized for credibility before the judge and the jury in their deliberations.

DOCUMENTATION AND COMMUNICATION

What documentation and communication is required in effective MOR? The emphasis must be for frank, accurate, fair, and consistent treatment throughout the MOR process. George Morrisey lists six common-sense steps to be followed by the supervisor in appraising and developing employees.

1. Know what you expect.
   a. Tasks, responsibilities, key results areas, or critical elements
   b. Performance standards, objectives, or assignments
2. Observe job performance.
3. Compare performance expectations with results.
4. Develop plan to improve performance results.

5. Use progress or development interview to motivate subordinates.

6. Carry out development plans and evaluate results.

Yes, these six steps are common sense, but common sense will also dictate that good documentation and the candid exchange of the development interview are essential. Good appraisal and development will only result from the commitment to best effort by the supervisor and the employee. Good feedback in this process will be a primary source of motivation as well as an opportunity to assure common understanding. What a unique opportunity for the supervisor to ask, "How do you feel we are doing jointly?" The employee's feedback could be invaluable to the development of both parties.

Proper documentation to support the MOR process and to prevent equal employment opportunity (EEO) exposures will include the following minimum considerations:

1. Review of reviewers.   Performance appraisal documents must be reviewed at least one organization level above the immediate reviewing supervisor. Performance appraisal and development of employees must be included in the evaluation of each level of supervision and management, i.e., each supervisor will be reviewed on how effective and timely that leader is in appraising, documenting results, and communicating with employees. Planning and reviewing personnel decisions before implementation is critical to preventing unfair, inconsistent personnel actions.

2. Application to all employees.   Documentation must be fair and consistent. Large, complex organizations can achieve fairness and consistency through training in the MOR process to develop this critical professional management skill with insistence on high standards of manager commitment to appraisal and development. Top-level managers must set a good example by demonstrating their skill and commitment in reviewing their immediate reporting managers, including reviewing how well they are appraising the next level of employees.

3. Judgment.   Significant incidents must be recorded in a "diary," both positive and negative. Do not trust to memory—an employee may get blame or credit for a fellow worker's error or achievement. The "diary" lets the employee know the supervisor is serious about his or her appraisal and development, and the employee is assured there will be no secrets or surprises. For the manager, the "diary" is invaluable, cutting down the agonizing preparation for timely review interviews. In the "diary," distinguish between the small but significant incidents and those events that fall into the category of "nitpicking." Discuss records with supervisors in other departments as a means of achieving uniformity throughout the company. (Be cautious of disclosing sensitive information.)

4. Accuracy and objectivity.   All documentation must be accurate and based on objective standards agreed to in advance, which apply to all employees. Statements must be true and correct to the best of the supervisor's knowledge—as if made under oath. Positive, constructive effort to support the employee's success must be clear in the documents. Too frequently a supervisor decides an employee must be discharged, then develops supporting "documentation" which is blatantly unfair—and damaging before the courts.

5. Timeliness.   Act promptly, putting all facts in writing while the facts are fresh in your memory. This will help to avoid appraisal review statements that emphasize only recent events and fail to review a full period of performance.

6. Communicate what you have written.   Let the employee know what you have recorded and listen to his or her version of what happened. Invite the employee's response. If significant, include the employee's remarks in the documentation.

7. Accesses to documentation.   All files that are used to determine qualifications for employment, promotion, additional compensation, or disciplinary action to and including discharge should be available to employees. (Note: California and other states provide by statute for employee access to these files.) Employee access to files is important because there should be no secrets and no surprises in the MOR process.

8. Expunge records.   When documentation is no longer useful or relevant, expunge your files of that data. With records of verbal or written warnings, when the documentation is no longer useful, tell the employee that the file has been expunged. The supervisor's act of forgiveness can motivate the employee to positive behavior.

CONCLUSION

For the professional manager, documentation and communication are basic skills—common-sense skills! The "teeth" in laws prohibiting discrimination highlight the urgency of assuring frank, accurate, fair, and consistent employee relations practices. We are past the time when business can condone untrained appraisers, indifferent attitudes toward performance appraisal responsibilities, or the "Mickey Mouse" scorecard evaluations of personality traits. Management's commitment to its people and to excellence in appraisal and development of human resources is now a high-priority managerial responsibility. Managers can no longer afford to stumble through discrimination minefields with skis on!

Bibliography

There have been many books written related to the subject matter in this text. I have selected here several that I have found particularly helpful and will make some brief remarks about each. That there are other books that are equally worthwhile (and many more that are not) is understood.

Batten, Joe. *Expectations and Possibilities.* Reading, Mass.: Addison-Wesley, 1981.

> An upbeat book by "Mr. Tough-Minded," this presents a strong philosophy, together with some realistic "how-tos," for establishing and achieving high expectations as an individual and as a manager who influences others. Chapter 11 deals with "The Expective Action Plan and Performance Appraisal System" and contains a series of insightful checklists and examples designed to help a supervisor maximize personal effectiveness in this responsibility.

Berg, J. Gary. *Managing Compensation.* New York: AMACOM, 1976.

> This book provides about as clear and concise a description of compensation systems from a lay point of view as any I have seen. For those interested in exploring the specifics of designing, implementing, and maintaining a workable approach to compensation, I thoroughly recommend it.

Blake, Robert R., and Mouton, Jane Srygley. *Productivity: The Human Side.* New York: AMACOM, 1981.

> This small book contains some of the most significant contributions (among many) that Blake and Mouton have made to management theory. They point out the powerful impact of group norms on human productivity and how a performance-oriented supervisor can use this insight to increase work group effectiveness.

Bolles, Richard N. *What Color Is Your Parachute? A Practical Manual for Job-Hunters & Career Changers.* Berkeley, Calif.: Ten Speed Press (updated annually).

> This truly classic book is an outstanding guide not only to someone who is seeking a job or career change but for anyone, such as a supervisor, who is interested in helping others plan for and attain their career goals.

Connellan, Thomas K. *How To Grow People Into Self-Starters.* Ann Arbor, Mich.: The Achievement Institute, 1980.

An innovative approach to human performance improvement is what this highly readable "manual" provides through what Tom Connellan refers to as a Self-Starting Mechanism. Unique features of the book are the appendix which includes "Key Learning Points," and "The Questions Answered" in each chapter which he recommends you review *first.*

Dailey, Charles A., and Madsen, Ann M. *How To Evaluate People in Business, The Track-Record Method Making Correct Judgments.* New York: McGraw-Hill, 1980.

Coming as a result of investigations for twenty-five organizations in both the public and private sectors over several years, this powerful book builds on the premise that "people should be judged on the basis of a documented 'track record' of results-producing performance." Chapter 2, "Let's Replace Performance Review," is an especially provocative treatise on redesign of traditional approaches to performance appraisal.

Drucker, Peter F. *Managing in Turbulent Times.* New York: Harper & Row, 1980, and *The Changing World of the Executive,* New York: Times Books, 1982.

These are two of the most recent books from the man who has made the greatest individual contribution to the philosophy and practice of management. Both are a series of essays by "St. Peter" and include some overlap between the two, portions of which were from articles in *The Wall Street Journal.* One, "A Scorecard for Management," appears in both and includes a very profound observation related to managerial performance and the "bottom line." "The bottom line measures *business* performance rather than *management* performance. And the performance of a business today is largely a result of the performance, or lack of it, of *earlier* managements in years past."

Giegold, William C. *Management By Objectives, A Self-Instructional Approach.* New York: McGraw-Hill, 1978.

Bill Giegold has developed an interesting, easy-to-follow approach to MBO in this colorful three-volume series, complete with some fascinating exercises applied to your own situation as well as some hypothetical cases. Volume III, which addresses Performance Appraisal, contains several interesting illustrations, including a table describing "The Elements of the Appraisal Process" in clear, concise terms.

Johnson, Robert G. *The Appraisal Interview Guide.* New York: AMACOM, 1979.

An excellent treatise on the art and science of appraisal interviews, this compact book expands on some significant communication concepts and techniques related to appraisal interviewing that can be used effectively by any supervisor.

Kellogg, Marion S. *What To Do About Performance Appraisal,* rev. ed. New York: AMACOM, 1975.

The original edition of this book was one of the first major works to address performance appraisals from a behavioral perspective. It had significant influence on subsequent publications, including mine. This edition expands on and validates many earlier perceptions, and provides a practical "how to" approach for managers. The chapters related to appraising potential and using appraisals for career counseling are especially insightful.

Mager, Robert F. *Goal Analysis* (1972); and Mager, Robert F., and Pipe, Peter. *Analyzing Performance Problems.* Belmont, Calif.: Fearon Pitman, 1970.

Never out of date, Bob Mager's books are fun to read but, more important, they pack a powerful message in easy-to-understand language. *Goal Analysis* is designed to help you take a broad statement of intent and remove it from "the land of Fuzz" so that "you will know one when you see one." *Analyzing Performance Problems,* subtitled "You Really Oughta Wanna," takes you through a series of basic questions to consider when someone is not performing satisfactorily. When the questions are answered, the solution is obvious—and it may not be the one that was obvious at the beginning. Read both of these books!

McConkey, Dale D. *Management By Objectives for Staff Managers.* New York: Vantage Press, 1972; and *MBO for Nonprofit Organizations.* New York: AMACOM, 1975.

Dale McConkey is one of the pioneers in MBO theory and practice. These two books are especially useful in helping managers in staff positions and in not-for-profit operations (including but not limited to governmental organizations) develop meaningful objectives and plans.

Morrisey, George L. *Management by Objectives and Results in the Public Sector,* 1976; and *Management by Objectives and Results for Business and Industry.* Reading, Mass.: Addison-Wesley, 1977; and *Getting Your Act Together: Goal Setting for Fun, Health and Profit.* New York: Wiley, 1980.

The first two books, of course, have been referenced liberally in this text and provide the management basis for this approach to performance appraisal. The third book is a jargon-free approach to using the concepts and techniques of MOR in all aspects of one's life and is especially useful in career development. In addition to the books, cassette learning programs on each of these subjects are available from MOR Associates, P.O. Box 5879, Buena Park, CA 90622.

Odiorne, George S. *MBO II: A System of Management Leadership for the 80s.* Belmont, Calif.: Fearon Pitman, 1979; and *The Change Resisters: How They Prevent Progress and What Managers Can Do About Them.* Englewood Cliffs, N.J.: Prentice-Hall, 1982.

Two of the latest books from the foremost proponent of MBO, the first takes a forward look at how a manager must adapt practices that have been successful in the past to methods designed to meet the changing requirements of the future. The second tells how people resist change and, more importantly, what individual managers can do about it in new and creative ways.

Steinmetz, Lawrence L. *Managing the Marginal and Unsatisfactory Performer.* Reading, Mass.: Addison-Wesley, 1969.

Still one of the most practical treatises on this sensitive and neglected area, this book is "must" reading for any supervisor faced with this kind of challenge (and who isn't?).

Stewart, Valeri, and Stewart, Andrew. *Practical Performance Appraisal.* Gower Press, England, 1977.

> Although written in the United Kingdom with a distinctly English flavor, this compact book provides some solid guidance on the effective installation of any performance appraisal system.

Ukeles, Jacob B. *Doing More With Less: Turning Public Management Around.* New York: AMACOM, 1982.

> An enlightened book primarily directed toward state and local government, this addresses head-on the mandate to public sector organizations to manage more effectively and efficiently. Drawn on the author's experience in dealing with the successful rescue of New York City from the brink of financial disaster, it has tremendous implications for performance management in the private as well as the public sector.